Allan Burnett is one of Scotland's best-selling authors for young readers. He was born and brought up in the Western Isles and educated at the University of Edinburgh, while working after dark as a ghost-tour guide. He has written many books, including *Mary, Queen of Scots and All That* and *Invented in Scotland – Scottish Ingenuity and Inventions through the Ages*. He is also the author of *World War I: Scottish Tales of Adventure* and *World War II: Scottish Tales of Adventure*.

THE STORY OF

Scotland

INSPIRED BY

THE GREAT TAPESTRY *of* SCOTLAND

ALLAN BURNETT

BIRLINN

First published in 2014 by
Birlinn Limited
West Newington House
10 Newington Road
Edinburgh
EH9 1QS

www.birlinn.co.uk

ISBN: 978 1 78027 241 2

British Library Cataloguing-in-Publication Data
A catalogue record for this book is available
from the British Library

Designed by James Hutcheson and Mark Blackadder
Typeset by Mark Blackadder

Printed and bound by
Bell and Bain Ltd, Glasgow

CONTENTS

INTRODUCTION

 A thread runs through this book. The thread of history. It binds together all that is contained inside.

Give it a tug by turning the pages, and it will take you away to other times, other places. To a lonely mountaintop where a climber cuts steps in the snow. To a firelit bedroom in a palace where a princess is born. And an ancient wood where a deer is stalked by a boy with a crossbow.

Follow the thread through the trees from coast to coast, out to sand-blasted islands and back into sweaty city wynds. Let it lead you down the gangway of a transatlantic ship, then yank you up into the sky on a clattering biplane, as you witness a thousand adventures over centuries and across continents.

In time, a recognisable pattern will emerge. It's the pattern of Scotland, a nation of the world, appearing before you in words and pictures.

The illustrations used in this book are details from the colourful wool and linen panels of The Great Tapestry of Scotland, which you can see in various towns and cities throughout the nation. You can find out if it's coming to a place near you by checking on the internet (www.scotlandstapestry. com).

The thread of this magnificent new tapestry – dreamt up by writers and artists, and made real by an army of stitchers – is the very same that will guide your journey.

Before setting off, you will need the following:

A comfortable seat.
A source of light
A bookmark.

Come on, there's no time to lose; let's join the story of Scotland. It begins at the beginning, the start of everything, millions of years ago.

The world back then is unrecognisable, inhospitable, alien. At least it is to humans. But don't worry, before you know it you will find your way.

Just keep hold of the thread . . .

THE EMPTY OCEAN

Imagine you are treading water in the sea. You look around. There is no beach nearby, nor land of any sort. It's just you and the Iapetus Ocean. It stretches off in every direction as far as the eye can see.

You are swimming in the exact spot where Scotland should be. Except this is 450 million years ago and Scotland doesn't exist yet. But don't worry, that's about to change. Gigantic land masses are going to appear and smash into each other with terrific force. If you stick around you will be pulverized. It won't be pretty. Luckily, you've got to be somewhere else.

The land takes shape

You're up in the sky, looking down. Volcanoes have spewed out amazing varieties of rock, and two land masses called Laurentia and Avalonia are colliding, causing the ground to crack. These cracks are known as 'faults'. They include the Great Glen and the Southern Upland Fault. Scotland is taking shape but it's still got a long way to go.

BEGINNING

THE JOURNEY NORTH

Hundreds of millions of years race past. Scotland is a swamp, a desert, a seabed and a volcanic hellhole that gets yanked around the Earth's crust. Finally, it cools and finds its proper place.

The time is now only 11,000 years ago. But no people actually live here yet. It's not hard to see why. The country is covered in an immense sheet of ice, about a mile high.

When the ice melts, scarring the landscape as it does so, people start to arrive from the warmer south. These are the early Scots, and they come here by walking across a great land bridge connecting Britain to the rest of Europe.

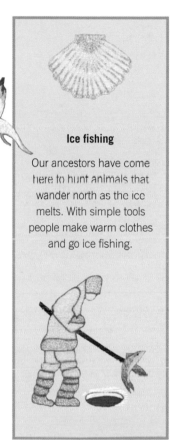

Ice fishing

Our ancestors have come here to hunt animals that wander north as the ice melts. With simple tools people make warm clothes and go ice fishing.

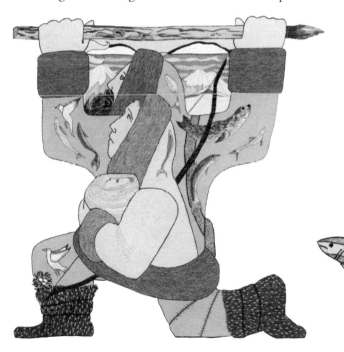

ANCIENT SCOTS

PEOPLE OF THE WILD WOOD

It is still more than 10,000 years ago and most of Scotland is a wild wood. Only the windswept Highland peaks rise above this damp jungle.

Watch out, there are dangers amid the trees. If you hear charging legs you'd better climb for it. The aurochs is a giant beast with horns two metres long, and the wild boar has tusks that can kill.

Wolves, wildcats and bears prey on the fish, waterfowl, otters and beavers that live in the streams, rivers and lochs.

The people of the wild wood hunt these creatures for food, adding deer and elk to the menu. They also gather vegetables, fruits and nuts.

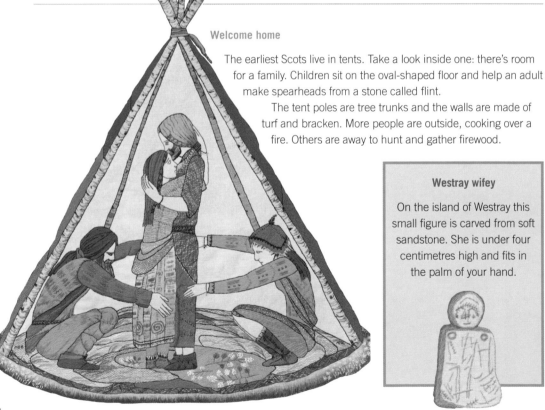

Welcome home

The earliest Scots live in tents. Take a look inside one: there's room for a family. Children sit on the oval-shaped floor and help an adult make spearheads from a stone called flint.

The tent poles are tree trunks and the walls are made of turf and bracken. More people are outside, cooking over a fire. Others are away to hunt and gather firewood.

Westray wifey

On the island of Westray this small figure is carved from soft sandstone. She is under four centimetres high and fits in the palm of your hand.

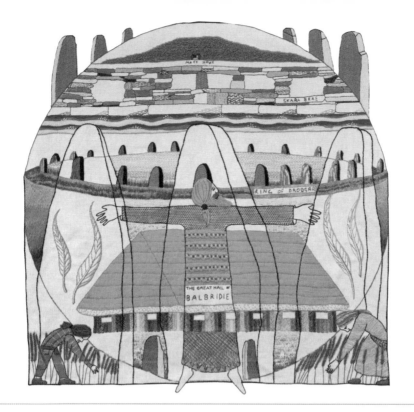

MYSTERY OF THE SKY GODS

It's 5,000 years ago. The land bridge to Europe has been flooded by the North Sea. Newcomers arrive in boats. The latest are farmers who grow crops like grain to make porridge. They keep animals in pens instead of chasing them around.

This makes the food supply more reliable so people have time to think about other things. Like, why does the sun and rain help things grow? Are the sun, clouds and stars gods we should worship? Farmers build stone monuments in order – perhaps – to celebrate such mysteries.

Protect and survive

Over time, homes become safer from attack. A crannog is a round house built on a wooden pier, protected by a loch. Its cone-shaped roof rests on a stone wall.

Weapons and tools

Weapons and tools are made from stone, wood, animal skins, bones, horns, and the antlers of deer and elk. A flint stone makes an axe head, a bone becomes a needle, a horn a drinking cup.

LAND OF

It's 320BC, and time to meet our first official tourist. His name is Pytheas, he travels by boat and he is Greek. The ancient Scots had visitors before now, but they left no surviving record of their journey.

Pytheas actually sets out from France, and sails around the whole island of Great Britain. When he reaches Scotland he takes a detour north to Orkney, Shetland and perhaps beyond. He also gives Britain a name – Pretannike – which means Land of the People with Tattoos. A colourful bunch.

Pytheas's boat

It's called a curragh and is made from animal skins stretched over a wooden frame. An expert local sailor sails it as far as he can. Then Pytheas gets off and catches another one.

The navigation stones

Pytheas visits the Isle of Lewis. At the stone circle of Calanais he uses a stick called a gnomon to measure how far north he has come.

THE FREE

THE SWORDSMAN FACES THE ROMANS

It's now 83 AD and three legions of Roman soldiers are marching into the heart of Scotland. The Roman Empire has conquered southern Pretannike – renaming it Britannica – and now they're here to try to conquer the north.

At a place called Mons Graupius the Roman leader, Agricola, faces a man they call Calgacus – 'the swordsman'.

Calgacus leads the Caledonians – the people of the land later called Scotland. Reports say that he gives a speech about the importance of freedom before his warriors clash with the invaders who would take that freedom away.

Spears fly and swords clank against shields. The Romans are victorious. But this is only one battle, and the surviving Caledonians are still free.

The frontier of Rome

The Romans fail to crush the Caledonians and instead build walls to keep them out. The first is ordered in AD 122 by emperor Hadrian. It separates most of present-day England, which has been conquered, from Scotland, which has not.

Another wall is built by the next emperor, Antoninus Pius, who tries to redraw the boundary of Roman Britain as a line between the Forth and Clyde rivers. But the Caledonians cause too much trouble and the Romans withdraw south again.

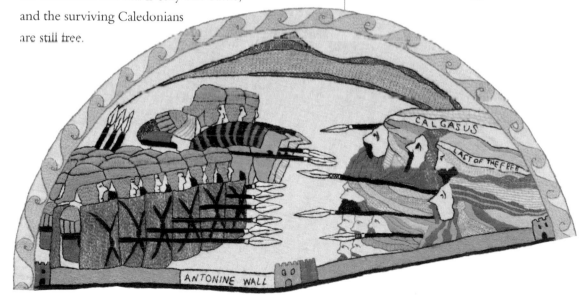

THE SAINT AND THE MONSTER

It is the year 563. Many boats have arrived on the island of Iona on Scotland's west coast. The sailors are on a mission from nearby Ireland. Their leader is a man called Columba.

Columba is an early Christian, and his mission is to spread the word of God. Many people in Scotland are pagans, which means that instead of worshipping God they believe in magic and pagan gods. Columba aims to change all that.

He and his followers travel to the mainland. They reach a riverbank where some pagans are burying one of their friends, whom they say was killed by a magical water beast.

To the pagans' astonishment, Columba instructs one of his followers to swim across the river. As he does so the young man is set upon by the water beast. Columba summons the power of God to scare the beast away. The pagans are impressed and Columba's mission is a success.

According to legend, the beast swims up river to Loch Ness – and becomes the famous Monster.

Mystical books and holy symbols

The Book of Kells is created on Iona in a church built by Columba's followers. It is written using fur brushes and quills made from bird feathers. These are dipped in ink made from crushed apples and iron paste. Christian stories and symbols are then scratched onto calf-skin pages. Similar symbols are carved into monuments such as the Ruthwell Cross near Dumfries.

THE GODS

The hermit in the cave

It is the fifth century. Inside a cave on a remote beach, Christian symbols are carved on the rock. The cave is on Scotland's south coast, near Whithorn. A holy man called Ninian reportedly comes here to pray.

Invaders known as Angles arrive from the south. Determined to stop them are the Picts, or 'painted ones', of Scotland. The Angles are led by King Ecgfrith, the Picts by King Bridei. In 685 they meet in battle at Dunnichen in central Scotland.

Footsoldiers holding shields are charged upon by cavalry. A second row of soldiers skewer the horses with long spears as the riders slam their swords down onto the frontline, aiming to split skulls. Ecgfrith is killed and the Angles retreat south.

15

VIKINGS

THERE'S A DRAGON ON THE BEACH

Huge, dragon-headed warships ride towards the shore on white crests of surf. Their menacing approach is spotted by Christian monks who drop their baskets, tools and fishing nets and run for their lives towards their monastery. But it's too late.

The invading longboats ram the pebble beach of Lindisfarne island. Sword-bearing warriors pour over the sides, splashing down in the shallows, capes hanging from their shoulders, heads and noses covered by battle helmets. They shout, they roar; some go mad – tearing off their shirts and biting the ends of their shields.

Each boat is dragged up the rasping shingle. Now the warriors give chase, thrusting blades into anyone who gets in their way. Blood-curdling screams put seabirds to flight.

Secrets of the longboats

After Lindisfarne, just by the border with England, the Vikings attack Skye and Iona in the west. They also sail far inland. But how? The secret is the longboats' draught – the bit under water. It's shallow, so the boats don't run aground even when rocks are near the surface. The longboats can also be dragged ashore and refloated in inland lochs.

The monastery doors crash open. Inside is treasure – Christian ornaments made from precious metals and jewels. The raiders remove the lot then search the island. They find plenty of food and drink to satisfy their appetites, and human slaves.

For this is just the beginning. There will be more monasteries to raid and one day fortresses, too, such as Dumbarton Rock. These attacks will threaten the very existence of Scotland. Right now, the year is 793 and you have just witnessed the arrival of the Vikings.

Scotland and Alba

From the 800s, Vikings seize the north-west coast and isles. For protection, the rest of Scotland unites as one kingdom. Various tribes once known as Caledonians, Picts, Scots, Britons and Angles are brought – peacefully or violently – together. At first the kingdom is known as Alba, then Scotland.

Cut to pieces

It's summer, 1018, and the kingdom is about to get bigger. Scottish axemen arrive at the River Tweed and hack up a force of English spearmen. The people of the Tweed are a mixed bunch, but they're now under Scottish rule.

THE CURSE

Night falls on a castle in the Highlands. A figure emerges from the gloom to stand in the castle courtyard. His name is Macbeth. This is his fortress and he is about to commit an infamous crime.

Padding up the steps to the guest bedchamber, Macbeth enters and pulls out a dagger from his cloak. As he stands over the sleeping body of Duncan, King of Scotland, Macbeth whispers, 'The deed must be done …' He then plunges the blade deep into Duncan's belly.

The king is dead – and the crown now belongs to Macbeth.

Three witches have persuaded Macbeth he can rule Scotland if he is prepared to destroy anyone who stands in his way. But his actions are about to have terrible consequences. Macbeth even kills his best friend, whose ghost returns to haunt him.

All of this means Macbeth is remembered as one of the cruellest kings ever. At least that's according to one version of Macbeth's life, made famous by William Shakespeare when his play about the Scottish king is first performed in 1606.

THRONE OF BLOOD

Scotland is not as bad as Shakespeare makes out, but it's still a dangerous job being king. Although the real-life Duncan isn't murdered, he meets a grisly end by being killed in battle – probably by subjects including Macbeth. Then there's the real Macbeth himself. His reign ends when Duncan's son, Malcolm, comes for revenge. At Lumphanan in Aberdeenshire there is a battle and Macbeth meets 'a cruel death'.

Facts not fiction

Let's take a closer look at the real Macbeth. He is born in the year 1005, or thereabouts, and grows up to be a successful leader in northern Scotland. In 1040 he becomes king and rules for 17 mostly peaceful years. In fact Macbeth's rule is so hassle-free he's able to leave on a Christian pilgrimage to Rome, where he gives money to the poor, then return to continue where he left off. So the real Macbeth is no witch-crazed murderer – though he does die a violent death.

'The golden one'

A song is written about the real Macbeth, which is part of a longer poem called *The Prophecy of Berchan*. In the song Macbeth is described as 'the red, tall, golden-haired one' whose reign has made Scotland prosper.

BEAUTY AND THE BEAST

King Malcolm III's nickname – Can More – means 'big head'. Maybe he feels really proud of himself. After all, he's just killed Macbeth, and Macbeth's stepson Lulach, to claim the throne. Or perhaps he actually has a huge noggin. If so, the crown might have to be made bigger.

And what Malcolm wants, Malcolm gets. In fact, according to some, he's a savage oaf who likes nothing better than fighting, feasting and chasing girlfriends.

Malcolm's most important girlfriend is Margaret, who is a calming influence. She becomes his wife in 1069, a year after the ship in which she is travelling is wrecked near North Queensferry. The couple have at least seven children who all grow up to be adults. They are lucky: a lot of children in the 11th century do not survive due to incurable illnesses.

THE GOOD SON TURNS BAD

The youngest son of Malcolm and Margaret is called David. In 1124 he becomes king. He does some good things during his reign. He sets up a lot of towns called Royal Burghs, and in these burghs people use coins to trade goods like wool and wine.

But David does some pretty nasty things, too. He invades northern England, burning houses and taking people as slaves. When a rebellion against him is launched up north, in the Highlands, David has the ringleaders rounded up and either imprisoned or executed. David then orders new castles to be built to keep his subjects in line. He also builds many important churches throughout Scotland.

SINNERS

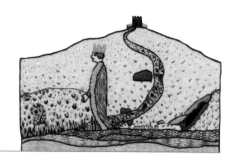

Palaces of prayer

Scotland's Border country is all forests, rivers and hills. The road is just a narrow track, the small houses made of wood and turf.

But what's this? Soaring above the treeline is a mighty stone structure. There's never been anything like it. You shout up to the builders working high overhead. They explain this is a church, one of the new abbeys ordered by King David.

St Andrew comes to Scotland

Back in the first century, St Andrew was a Christian Apostle who knew Jesus Christ. After St Andrew died some of his bones were brought to Scotland. These include three finger bones, an upper arm bone, a kneecap and a tooth. In the 1100s a grand cathedral is built to house them and the place becomes known as St Andrews.

HERE COMES HAAKON

It's autumn 1263. Warships have entered the Firth of Clyde, around 150 in all. At the prow of one especially large vessel is a gilded dragon's head. The Vikings are back.

Actually, they never left. The kings of Norway have ruled northwest Scotland and the isles for hundreds of years. But now their power is slipping. Scottish king Alexander II and, later, his son Alexander III have been attacking Norse lands to try to unite them with the rest of the kingdom.

On board the Viking flagship is Haakon, elderly King of Norway. He's determined Norse Scotland remains under his control. His fleet moors off Cumbrae Island, near the mainland settlement of Largs.

A storm whips up and some Norse ships are forced ashore. The army of Alexander III has been lying in wait. Now they attack until night falls.

Next day, Haakon leads the reinforcements. Arrows, spears and stones fly. Men and horses clash on the beach. The Norsemen are forced back. Many of them are slain, turning the Atlantic waters red with their blood.

VIKINGS

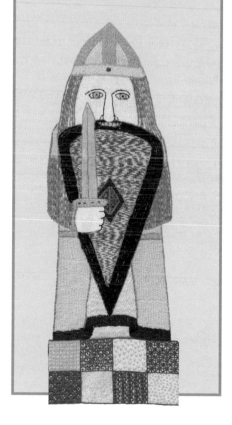

THE SHRINKING EMPIRE

Haakon survives the Battle of Largs. He retreats through the Hebrides to the Northern Isles. He plans to spend winter at the Bishop's Palace in Kirkwall, Orkney, before returning to Norway. But Haakon is sick, perhaps injured, and dies at the palace. The Hebrides and other lands are sold to Scotland.

Somerled

Somerled is a Scottish Viking with Norse ancestors. He is the Lord of the Isles and his men patrol the west coast in warships called birlinns. These ships are based on traditional Viking longboats, which had a steer-board on their right-hand side. This is where the word 'starboard' comes from.

Birlinns are a bit different. They have a rudder at the stern (back). This makes them more nimble when Somerled orders an attack.

THE KING IS DEAD

The night of 19 March 1286 is truly dark and stormy. King Alexander III sits feasting in Edinburgh Castle, but he's restless. He wants to be with his young French bride, Yolande. The trouble is, Yolande is miles away in Kinghorn Castle on the other side of the Firth of Forth, the finger of sea that separates Edinburgh from Fife.

The King orders a horse and gallops into the night, his belly full of wine. He reaches the shore at South Queensferry – named after the earlier Queen Margaret – and is ferried to the north side.

Alexander's horse picks its way along Fife's cliff tops. But its rider is unsteady and the gusts too strong.

Suddenly the horse slips and plunges, king and all, onto the beach below. Alexander is found the next morning – dead – with a broken neck.

INDEPENDENCE

THE MAID

The heir to the throne is Alexander's granddaughter, a little girl called Margaret. Known as the Maid of Norway, she is brought over to Scotland but dies during the voyage.

ENTER LONGSHANKS

There are now many rival claims to the throne, but no clear heir. The Scots need someone to judge who should be king. So they turn to the neighbouring King of England, Edward Longshanks.

Longshanks picks John Baliol to be Scotland's new king and starts pushing him around. Baliol goes along with this for a while but then tells Edward he's had enough.

A furious Edward invades Scotland, gets rid of Baliol and seizes the throne for himself – which has been his plan all along. Now the Scots must fight for their independence

> ### Stone of Destiny
>
> The Stone of Destiny, an oblong block of red sandstone, is a national treasure. Each new Scottish monarch must sit on it to be crowned.
>
> During Longshanks's invasion the stone is taken from Scone Abbey, near Perth, to London. Only 700 years later is it permanently returned to Scotland.

WILLIAM

THE REBEL ALLIANCE

It's 1296. English soldiers patrol the land and locals are brutally pushed around. Two men decide to do something about it.

The first is Andrew Murray, who leads a rebellion in the north against English rule. He is joined by William Wallace, a rebel in the south.

We don't know much about Murray, but Wallace is a low-ranking Ayrshire nobleman. The story goes that Wallace is harassed by English soldiers, who kill his father and steal his possessions, so he fights back.

With the help of his wife, Mirren, Wallace evades capture. But Mirren is punished by the local Sheriff, William Heselrig, who has her executed.

Swearing revenge, Wallace goes to Heselrig's house one night and kills him. There's no turning back. Wallace is now an outlaw and, along with a band of followers, joins Murray's rebellion.

RISE AND FALL

In 1297, Wallace and Murray spectacularly defeat the English army at the Battle of Stirling Bridge. The two men are made Guardians of Scotland, but Murray dies of his wounds.

Wallace is then defeated by the English at the Battle of Falkirk in 1298. He continues to campaign for Scottish independence, and visits the King of France around 1300 to try to enlist his support.

The French king is sympathetic, but to no avail. Wallace is eventually betrayed to the English and captured in 1305. He is taken to London where Longshanks has him tortured and executed.

WALLACE

Battle of Stirling Bridge

This battle of 1297 is where Wallace and Murray defeat the invading English. So how do they do it?

The Scots are greatly outnumbered and should have no chance. But Wallace and Murray have picked a brilliant location, the bridge over the River Forth near Stirling.

Stirling Bridge is narrow and the English army large. When the English cross the bridge to meet their enemy, they are squeezed together because there's so many of them and soon get in a muddle.

The Scots attack and chaos breaks out in the English ranks. Retreating English soldiers try to

go back across the bridge but are crushed against their colleagues who are still pressing forward.

The bridge collapses under the weight and many poor souls drown, weighed down by their armour and chain mail. The rest are killed or taken prisoner by the victorious Scots.

Blind Harry

Wallace's story is made famous in later medieval times by a minstrel called Blind Harry. Accompanied by a harp, Harry sings of Wallace's heroic deeds, his torture and execution.

Blind Harry's story of Wallace – which mixes historical fact with fiction – becomes a printed book in the 1500s.

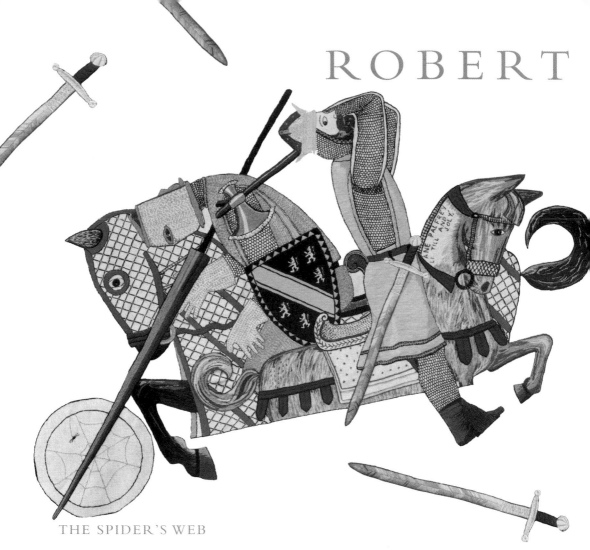

THE SPIDER'S WEB

It is the winter of 1306–7. On an island off Scotland's west coast you find a cave where a man is hiding. He looks gloomy, but then spots a spider hanging by a glistening thread.

The spider struggles to make its web, but eventually succeeds. The man takes heart and vows that he, too, will succeed with the task that is troubling him.

But is what you see for real?

In fact, the spider and its web are probably a myth. It is a story told to embroider the facts, like adding embroidery to a tapestry.

Yet the man is real. He's King Robert the Bruce. He is hiding out with relatives in the isles and is feeling pretty low. Although he's been crowned king and has taken up the cause of Scottish independence following Wallace's execution, many Scots do not want him. He has been chased away and Longshanks still rules Scotland.

The Bruce vows to fight back, win Scots' support and drive the English out of Scotland.

THE BRUCE

BANNOCKBURN

Midsummer, 1314. By a river called the Bannock Burn, near Stirling, two armies are camped. Their colourful tents and flags ripple in the breeze.

Leading one side is King Robert the Bruce, who has taken up the cause of Scotland.

The other army is at least twice as big. It's led from behind by England's Edward II, weak son of the late, great Longshanks.

Suddenly, an English knight charges at Bruce with his lance. Bruce sidesteps his pony at the last moment and smashes the knight's skull with his battleaxe.

The armies clash. The English cavalry get bogged down and skewered by Scots spearmen, causing chaos. Arrows from the English side strike the backs of their own men. Edward flees and the English retreat. It's a Scottish victory.

For castle and country

The Battle of Bannockburn has been fought to decide the fate of this mighty fortress. By winning, the Bruce secures the surrender of the English garrison.

Thanks to the Bruce and his allies, the English invasion is a failure and soon Scotland is an independent kingdom again.

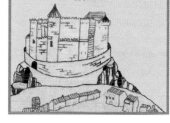

DECLARATION OF INDEPENDENCE

The magic box

The Bruce orders a small metal box to be brought to Bannockburn. They say it contains the bones of St Columba, who defeated wizards and monsters. The Scots soldiers believe it can help them win, and it does.

The Bruce becomes a hero, but if he fails to rule properly the Scots will select a new king. This is stated in The Declaration of Arbroath in 1320, one of several letters also declaring Scotland's independence.

A PLAGUE ON ALL OUR HOUSES

It is 1348 and a terrifying disease is sweeping through Europe. They call it the Black Death. They say it started in China and now it has arrived in England. Millions of people, young and old, are either dead or dying.

The Black Death is also known as the bubonic plague. People catch it when they are bitten by infected fleas. The disease attacks the victim's glands and enters their bloodstream. Within a few days they are usually dead.

There is another kind of plague, called the pneumonic plague. It is spread through the air rather than by touch.

People understand little or nothing about the disease and its effects. Many Scots even imagine that they are immune – they cannot be infected – as the plague will only attack the English and stop at the border. But they are wrong.

The rats

Bubonic plague is carried by fleas that live in the fur of rats. Contact with the rats means death because the fleas will easily jump from the rats onto human skin.

Since people don't understand the disease, it makes their fear of catching it all the greater. Some view it as a punishment from God.

BLACK DEATH

The soldiers' curse

You're in a village in the Borders. A soldier runs towards you, shouting: 'The Black Death of the English!' You can see the terror in his eyes. More people follow, pouring out of the woods.

You must hide. For the Scottish army have just attacked northern England only to find themselves infected with the plague.

Ring-a-ring o' roses

'Ring a ring o' roses,
A pocket full of posies,
A tishoo! A tishoo!
We all fall down.'

This popular singing game is said to describe the effects of the plague, but it was probably invented much later than the 14th century.

Empty lands

You stumble upon a cottage. It seems deserted except for a young farm hand.

'Want to know something?' he says. 'The old farm workers have died of the plague. The farm needs me, so they pay double.'

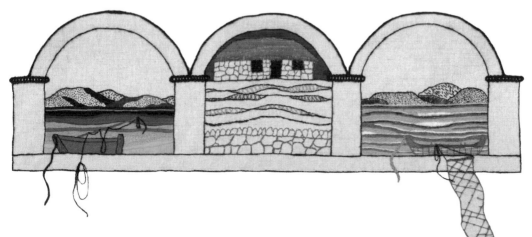

THE FIRST UNIVERSITY

The year is 1413 and you meet a young man at an inn on the highway. Where is he going?

'I'm off to the new university at St Andrews,' he says. 'I can't wait. My older brother sailed abroad to study in Paris. Luckily I don't have to.'

A bearded man holding a tankard of ale joins the conversation. 'But what about Oxford or Cambridge down south?' he says.

'Haven't you heard?' says the young scholar with a laugh. 'We've been fighting the English on and off for more than a hundred years. No-one wants to go down there. It's much better to have our own university here in Scotland.'

LEARNING

THE SEEDS OF KNOWLEDGE

If the human world is to progress, it needs educated people to make it happen. The Scots know this, and as a result, four universities are built in Scotland during medieval times.

After St Andrews in 1413 comes Glasgow in 1451, then Aberdeen four years later and finally Edinburgh in 1583. Some students are very young. It's not unusual to see boys aged ten attending lectures. You can spot them, in Glasgow for example, wearing distinctive gowns.

Girls are not allowed to study, and that situation does not change for hundreds of years. So you can see there's still a long way to go when it comes to progress.

The smartest dunce

Even before Scotland builds its first universities, the nation produces some exceptionally clever people. One of them is a philosopher called John Duns Scotus.

Born in Berwickshire around 1265, Duns Scotus travels widely in order to learn. He studies and teaches at Oxford and Cambridge in England, and Paris in France. Duns Scotus helps people understand more about how our minds work, about who or what God is, and about how the universe is created.

For a long time after his death, Duns Scotus is misunderstood. People even start using the name 'Dunce' (another way of writing Duns) as an insult, meaning a stupid person. But as time goes by he becomes regarded as one of medieval Europe's great thinkers.

33

JAMES III

MARGARET of DENMARK

HOW NOT TO RULE

It's the 1480s and things are not looking good for King James III. He's let criminals get away with murder, increased taxes and hoarded the cash, and ordered the royal mint to forge a load of worthless coins. Plus, the servant who used to sew his shirts has been given one of the kingdom's top jobs – Archbishop of St Andrews.

Many powerful nobles are furious. The king is arrested at Lauder in the Borders and several of his favourites are hanged from the local bridge. But on his release, James carries on as before. He should have learned his lesson: in 1488, at a battle near Stirling Castle, he's killed by rebels led by his own son.

MIGHTY FALL

Riches of the Isles

In spite of his failings, James III has some success. Thanks to his marriage to Margaret, daughter of the King of Denmark and Norway, the Northern Isles and their rich fishing grounds are brought under Scottish rule.

HERRING BUSS

The thistle and the rose

In 1503 James IV marries English royal Margaret Tudor, thus marrying Scotland's thistle to England's rose. But the honeymoon between the two warring kingdoms doesn't last.

DAWN OF THE DOOMED

In the half-light of dawn you see bodies every-where, thousands of them. Many are already dead but others are slowly dying in agonising pain. Most are Scots. They came here to Flodden Field to do battle with the English.

It should have been a brilliant Scottish triumph. The downhill charge was led by James IV, the warrior king who had slain his own father in battle then made the kingdom prosper after years of misrule. Now the king and his nobles lie here, defeated and lifeless.

You had better lie down, too, and play dead: a group of English soldiers are coming, waving their torches around, looking for plunder. They will remember 1513 as a great year.

THE PRINTING PRESS

Before James IV dies, Scotland is changed forever. In 1508 a new machine appears in Edinburgh called a printing press. It's producing magical new objects called printed books, each one a perfect copy of the last.

No more will scribes be required to painstakingly copy texts by hand. No more will knowledge be the property of a chosen few. Most people still cannot read. But that will change with books. Everything will change with books.

You arrive at the Cowgate, a bustling thoroughfare in the steeply sloping valley south of Edinburgh's High Street. Here are the premises of Walter Chepman and his business partner, Andrew Myllar, a bookseller who has learned the art of printing in France. Together these men are publishing Scotland's first printed books.

BOOKS

Entering the shop, you see the printing press and take one of the completed volumes in your hand. Its cover smells strongly of animal skin, its neatly chopped pages bristle against your fingertips. The perfect lines of words created by the machine's metal type are a marvel.

The price of each book has been set by James IV himself. In 1507, the King granted Chepman and Myllar permission to set up their venture and he continues to take a close interest in the new technology.

Chepman and Myllar's business lasts only a few years, but in time other Scottish printing presses are set up and the books keep coming.

Book of the Howlat

One of Scotland's earliest printed books, made in 1508, is called *The Book of the Howlat*. It tells the story of an owl – or 'howlat' – who is unhappy with his appearance.

The owl asks the leader of all birds, the peacock, to make him better looking. The owl is granted more feathers but becomes too full of pride, so he's stripped of his new plumage.

Ink and vellum

The Chepman and Myllar printing press uses technology introduced to Europe around 1450 by German blacksmith Johannes Gutenberg.

To print each page, the press, which is made of wood, pushes carefully arranged metal letters – or type – against a piece of paper.

The ink used in the process is made with oil, a bit like varnish. This means it sticks to the page and doesn't run. The pages are often made from paper, but upmarket editions use vellum – stretched calfskin.

THE

PALACES OF WONDER

It is 1538 and in the elegant courtyard of Linlithgow Palace, west of Edinburgh, you find stonemasons are hard at work crafting a magnificent fountain decorated with statues of unicorns, mermaids and a lion.

Built for King James V, who was born at the palace in 1512, this splendid structure is a prime example of the Renaissance – an age of great works of literature, art and architecture which started in Italy and influenced the whole of Europe.

Renaissance culture has been flowering in Scotland for some time. It was promoted by James V's father, James IV, who encouraged such innovations as the printing press and whose court was entertained by poets, musicians and scholars. Now James V is taking things to a new level.

Along with Linlithgow, James V spends a fortune on a lavish palace at Stirling Castle and extensive improvements to Falkland Palace – including building a tennis court there in 1539.

Play in the open air

Walking among the trees near Cupar, Fife, in 1552 you hear voices in a nearby field. It's a play being performed outside.

Known as *The Thrie Estaitis*, this popular piece of drama, about nobles, the church and the common people, is a fine example of Scotland's Renaissance culture.

RENAISSANCE

The French connection

Meet the glamorous wife of James V. Her name is Mary of Guise, a member of a prestigious French family. The couple's marriage is seen as a boost for Scotland because France is a powerful kingdom at the cutting edge of Renaissance fashions.

French masons, craftsmen and decorators are responsible for much of the building work on James and Mary's royal palaces. In these grand residences the couple preside over their colourful court – an international gathering of artists, musicians and scholars – and dine on delicious food and fine French wine.

An economic law

Building Renaissance palaces is an expensive business, and by 1532 King James V is already short of cash. He therefore sends a message to the Pope asking if he can keep some of the Church income that normally gets sent to Rome.

'You can keep 10,000 gold ducats,' the Pope says, 'but on one condition: you must set up a new law court based on Roman law.'

James agrees and establishes the Court of Session – a cornerstone of the modern Scots legal system.

FLAMES OF REVOLUTION

It's a cold February day in 1528 and on the street outside a church in St Andrews a man is being tied to a thick pole of wood called a stake. A fire is lit beneath him and slowly the smoke and flames begin to envelop his body. His lips move in prayer but people can see he is in agony.

Patrick Hamilton is being executed for heresy – that is, for challenging the authority of the Bishops and the Pope, who run the Church. Hamilton is one of thousands of men across Europe who have been protesting at the way the Church is managed.

These protestors, or Protestants, say Church leaders are not up to the job. They are greedy and selfish, using the vast wealth of the Church to buy luxuries for themselves while many common folk live in poverty.

This criticism includes the royal household. The king's lavish palaces are regarded by Protestants as an ungodly extravagance, as meanwhile the common people are kept ignorant of Renaissance culture – unable even to read the Bible for themselves.

The Protestants want a reorganisation – or Reformation – of the Church. They want ordinary people to be taught to read the Word of God.

The existing Church authorities are horrified by such prospects. They hope that executing Hamilton will make people afraid to follow his example. But instead, Hamilton's death causes a lot of sympathy and more Scots become Protestants.

REFORMATION

THE NEW SCOTLAND

In 1560 the Reformation finally
sweeps the old
Church from power
and Scotland is declared
a Protestant country. Beautiful
monasteries, abbeys and other
buildings of the old Church are ransacked
or destroyed.

Despite this, most common folk are still with the old
Church, but the Reformation has taken root in Edinburgh
among the kingdom's most powerful people.

Many Reformers are committed Protestants but others
are greedy nobles who go along with it so they can grab
some Church lands and riches for themselves. Some
things never change.

John Knox

Edinburgh is gripped by Reformation fever and you are in a
packed city church. An angry-looking man in black robes with a
long beard is preaching.

His name is John Knox. He used to be a priest until he rebelled
against the Church and ended up being imprisoned on a French
warship. For two years he was chained to an oar and whipped
when he didn't row fast enough.

Eventually Knox was freed and returned home to lead the
Scottish Reformation.

MARY, QUEEN

ESCAPE FROM HOME

Snow falls on Linlithgow Palace where fire-lit rooms echo with the cries of a newborn girl. It's December 1542 and the baby daughter of Mary of Guise is crowned queen, aged just six days. Her father, James V, has died at the age of thirty.

The girl's name? Mary, Queen of Scots.

King Henry VIII of England wants Mary married to his son. When powerful Scots resist, Henry attacks Scotland in what becomes known as the 'Rough Wooing' of Mary.

For safekeeping the five-year-old queen is sent to her mother's country, France, where she is married to Prince François. Together they become king and queen of France.

But when François dies suddenly, his family don't want Mary around any more.

OF SCOTS

MURDER AND REBELLION

Mary returns to Scotland in 1561. Living at Holyrood Palace, the teenage queen is constantly bullied by nobles and churchmen.

A new husband is needed to strengthen Mary's rule by giving her an heir. So in 1565 she marries her handsome cousin, Lord Darnley.

Apart from fathering Mary's son — the future James VI — Darnley is a disaster: rude, arrogant and violent. He joins a gang who murder Mary's favourite servant David Rizzio in front of her at Holyrood.

When Darnley himself is also killed in 1567, Mary's situation spins out of control. Still clinging to the old Catholic religion, Mary is removed from power by powerful Protestant nobles.

Along with her crown, Mary has to give up her baby, James VI. She flees to safety in England and ends up in the captivity of another cousin, Queen Elizabeth I.

Eventually, Elizabeth suspects Mary of plotting against her. In 1587, at Fotheringhay Castle, Mary is executed.

Who killed Darnley?

On 10 February, 1567, the body of Lord Darnley is discovered in a garden next to his Edinburgh residence. The building has been blown up, yet there are no blast marks on his body. There's a dagger on the grass — but no stab wounds.

It's likely Darnley escaped the bomb in the nick of time, used the dagger for defence, but was caught and strangled.

So who killed him? The chief suspect is the Earl of Bothwell, who turns out to be Mary's new lover and third husband. He had good reason for wanting Darnley out of the way.

Queen of disguises

One of Mary's favourite pastimes is wearing masks and disguises. She even goes to Stirling dressed as a beggar to see what a poor person's life is like.

RAIDERS AND

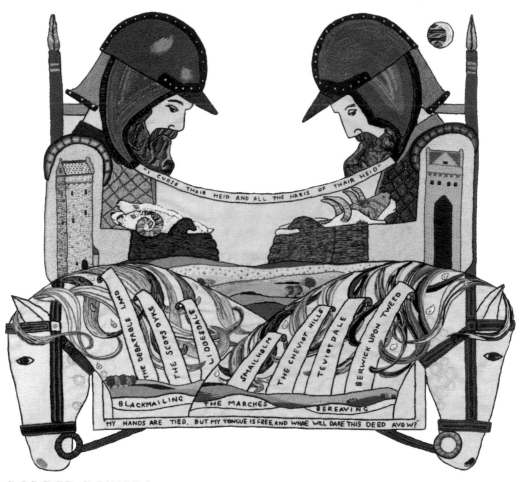

"I CURSE THAIR HEID AND ALL THE HARIS OF THAIR HEID"

THE DEBATABLE LAND · THE SCOTS DYKE · LIDDESDALE · SMAILHOLM · THE CHEVIOT HILLS · TEVIOTDALE · BERWICK UPON TWEED

BLACKMAILING · THE MARCHES · BEREAVING

MY HANDS ARE TIED, BUT MY TONGUE IS FREE, AND WHAE WILL DARE THIS DEED AVOW?

BORDER REIVERS

You are in a Borders forest in the late 1500s when a group of armed men thunders past, followed by others in hot pursuit. The men are from rival local clans known as Border Reivers – meaning raiders.

Like the clans of the Highlands, the Reivers steal from each other and from passers-by. Time to make yourself scarce.

Reiving, or raiding, has gone on for centuries, encouraged by many

cross-border wars between England and Scotland. Army after army has passed through here, helping themselves to people's homes, farms and animals. With little left, Border clans such as the Kerrs, Scotts and

RUSTLERS

Armstrongs long ago resorted to robbery to survive.

The bloody Battle of Flodden in 1513 caused havoc in the Borders. Then came the 'Rough Wooing' of Mary, Queen of Scots and the turmoil of her reign, bringing up more English armies to cause yet more destruction.

Neither the Scottish nor English government upholds the law here. So it's up to locals armed with swords, spears, shields and ridged helmets called 'morions' to make their own rules.

WILLIE ARMSTRONG

It's 1596 and Kinmont Willie Armstrong, a ruthless and violent Scottish reiver, is imprisoned in Carlisle Castle on the English side of the border.

Armstrong had been captured on what was supposed to have been a 'truce day' – a day when nobody can be arrested, not even criminals. But the Reiver law was ignored, and Armstrong captured by a group of English riders.

Suddenly rescuers appear, taking the guards by surprise. The jail's door is forced open and Armstrong is bundled out, free to live and rob another day.

Highland rustlers

Like the Borders, the Highlands and Islands in the 1500s is a wild region that's often beyond government control. Rival clans are regularly at loggerheads and steal each other's animals.

Two exceptional clans are the MacDonalds and the Campbells, each controlling many smaller clans who fight for them. One of the most notorious of the smaller clans is the MacGregors.

The MacGregors are considered so awful that the entire clan is outlawed in 1603 to try to force them to change their ways. But old habits die hard. More than a century later, in the early 1700s, MacGregors such as Rob Roy continue to seize others' cattle at gunpoint.

THE BOY KING

In the summer of 1583 the 17-year-old son of Mary, Queen of Scots rides into St Andrews after escaping from Ruthven Castle near Perth, where he's been imprisoned for almost a year. At the earliest opportunity, he has his kidnappers exiled or executed.

This tough and ruthless young man, James VI of Scotland, is also the most important ruler in British history. He reigns for an amazing 58 years, during which time he brings the wild Border Reivers under control.

James is also a scholar who publishes a new edition of the Bible. He writes books explaining why he is the most important person in the kingdom and why people shouldn't smoke tobacco.

But the main reason for James's importance is this: he is the first monarch to rule over all of Britain. Upon the death of England's Elizabeth I in 1603, he inherits her throne and becomes James I of England, Wales and Ireland.

King James Bible

Being a scholarly king, James VI and I orders a new version of the Bible to be translated into English from Greek and Hebrew scriptures.

JAMES VI

UNION OF THE CROWNS

On 24 March, 1603, English courtier Sir Robert Carey rides north from London. He makes it to the Scottish border in just two days. Exhausted, he falls off his horse, which kicks him. Eventually he staggers into Holyrood Palace and demands to see King James.

From his pocket Carey produces a ring, originally a gift from James to England's Elizabeth I. It has been pulled from the queen's finger upon her death and brought to James as a message that her throne is now his.

James succeeds to Elizabeth's throne because she had no children. Through his father, Lord Darnley, and his great-grandmother Mary Tudor in particular, James has the strongest claim of inheritance.

He moves to London to reign as James I and revisits Scotland only once, in 1617, where he remains James VI. Although one king now has two crowns, Scotland and England remain separate kingdoms.

Ulster Scots

As the Protestant king of Great Britain and Ireland, James sees an opportunity to destroy two enemies at once. He wants rid of the Border Reivers, and he wants to crush Catholicism in Ireland.

So he sends Reiver clans from the Borders to a part of Ireland called Ulster, and tells them to make a home for themselves by driving out the native Catholics. These reivers later become known as Ulster Scots.

THOU SHALT NOT SUFFER A WITCH TO LIVE

AGNES SAMPSON

JOHN FIAN

BURNED AT THE STAKE

It's 1608, and something wicked is going on in Edinburgh. 'Come and see the witches burn!' shouts a little boy as he runs past and up the narrow city street. You follow and find a large crowd has gathered to watch the gruesome spectacle.

A group of at least half a dozen women have been tied to stakes – strong wooden posts – and fires lit under them. Some onlookers are cheering, some are chanting, and a few are weeping. As the smoke and flames intensify, some of the women cry out in agony.

Suddenly, three of them break free – the ropes tying them to the stakes have been burnt through. With horribly burned skin the women try to stagger away, but members of the crowd grab them and throw them back into the fire.

Why are these women being burned alive? People believe them to be witches and they must be punished accordingly. But are they really guilty?

WIZARDS

THE WITCH-HUNT

During Reformation times, witches are hunted all over Europe. Witches are believed to be Devil-worshippers who curse other people with misfortune. Scotland's witch-hunt begins in 1563, when a law is passed by the kingdom's new Protestant government outlawing witchcraft on pain of death.

Some of those accused of witchcraft are actually healers or midwives, who help deliver babies. Many are accused because of a quarrel with a neighbour, or unkind gossip. The accused are tortured until they confess to terrible crimes that actually never happened.

The witch craze eventually results in the deaths of hundreds of Scottish women – and some men, too.

Wizard or scientist?

One man suspected of dabbling in witchcraft, or wizardry, is John Napier of Merchiston, near Edinburgh. Born in 1550, Napier is a wealthy laird who believes one of his servants is a thief. In order to find the guilty person, Napier tells all his servants to enter a darkened room, one by one, and stroke the cockerel perched inside. The cockerel, he declares, will know when it is stroked by the thief – and tell its master.

When Napier later identifies the culprit, the servants believe it is witchcraft. They don't know Napier coated the cockerel in soot. He knew the thief would not risk stroking the bird, and all he had to do was pick out the servant whose hands were still clean.

So Napier is really more scientist than sorcerer. Among his many brilliant inventions is an early computing system that uses ivory counting rods known as Napier's Bones.

1ST MARQUIS OF MONTROSE

SIR DAVID LESLIE

THE GREAT MONTROSE

Gunfire rings out across the misty field of Philiphaugh, near Selkirk, on 13 September 1645. The Marquis of Montrose, a brilliant general who has brought his army here for battle, is taken by surprise.

Montrose's opponent, General Sir David Leslie, has cunningly divided his force into two to attack Montrose's men from in front and behind. Montrose fights bravely, but when it becomes clear the day is lost he is persuaded to flee to fight another day.

Leslie is a Covenanter – a group of Scots who oppose the king, Charles I, because of his attempts to make the Scottish Protestant Church more like the English one.

Montrose is a Royalist – he used to be a Covenanter until he decided they were too severe. He switched sides to become a staunch defender of the king.

By upsetting not only the Scottish Covenanters but also a lot of powerful Englishmen and Irishmen, Charles I has triggered a civil war. It is this war that has pitched Montrose against Leslie.

Montrose has won many battles but after defeat at Philiphaugh he is exiled to Germany and Scandinavia. In 1649, upon discovering Charles I has been executed by English rebels, Montrose vows revenge. He returns to Scotland only to be captured and executed in Edinburgh in 1650.

CIVIL WAR

THE NATIONAL COVENANT

In 1638 a crowd gathers in Greyfriars Kirkyard, Edinburgh, to sign the National Covenant – a document proclaiming the independence of the Scottish Church. They become known as the Covenanters.

COVENANTERS' MONUMENT

The Killing Times

After Charles I's death, Scotland is invaded by English leader Oliver Cromwell who rules for almost a decade. Then, in 1660, royalty is restored under Charles II, who hunts down all who opposed his executed father – including Covenanters.

By the 1680s, government troops are hanging Covenanters from the trees. They call it 'the Killing Times'

In Wigtown Bay in 1685, two Covenanter women are tied to stakes where the tide is flooding in. One of them, Margaret Wilson, is just a girl. She wriggles to try to keep her head above water, but there is no escape.

Masked preacher

Covenanters such as preacher Alexander Peden are outlawed by Charles II. This requires Peden to defend and disguise himself. So he buckles on a sword belt, holsters with pistols, a face mask and a wig.

Island prison

In the 1670s Covenanters are imprisoned on the Bass Rock, a tiny barren island in the Firth of Forth.

IN SEARCH OF AN EMPIRE

It is July 1698. Five ships carrying 1,200 people are setting out from Edinburgh's port of Leith. Ahead of them is a voyage of more than 5,000 miles across the Atlantic Ocean.

Their ultimate destination is a place called Darien, on the Isthmus of Panama, a narrow strip of land that links North and South America with the Atlantic and Pacific Oceans on either side.

The plan is to make Darien a gateway for trade between continents. Ships' cargoes can pass through it – for a fee – instead of making the very long and dangerous journey around the tip of South America.

If successful the venture could greatly improve Scotland's fortunes. Many Scots have gone hungry because of harvest failures,

DISASTER

while the English have undermined Scotland's trade with other countries. England, meanwhile, has grown wealthy and powerful thanks to its trade in Asia, Africa and America.

The Darien scheme, proposed by William Paterson, is therefore seen by Scots as the key not only to becoming better off, but to catching up with their rich neighbour by building a Scottish empire.

As a mark of their ambitions the settlers propose to call the Darien colony 'New Caledonia' after the ancient name for Scotland.

WELCOME TO THE JUNGLE

Finally, after a voyage of almost four months, the Scottish ships arrive at Darien. But the land of their dreams turns out to be a dangerous, inhospitable place. In summer, the heat in its tropical jungles is unbearable.

The adventurers' lack of knowledge, skills and experience means they build a settlement in the wrong place and are unable to grow crops to feed themselves. Food supplies rot and deadly insects attack. People die of hunger and disease at the rate of ten a day.

A second expedition of a thousand Scots arrives, but many of these, too, meet their doom. Rival Spanish colonists attack and the whole settlement has to be abandoned. Only a few hundred live to tell the tale.

The aftermath

The sum of £400,000 – an enormous amount of money in the 1690s – has been raised from Scottish investors to pay for Darien. When the scheme collapses, the money is lost.

Darien is such a disaster, it virtually guarantees Scotland will have to join a closer union with England in order to survive. It also ensures that many Scots will lack the confidence to run their own affairs for centuries to come.

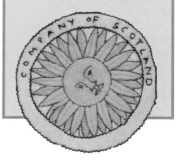

A PARCEL

THE UNION WITH ENGLAND

From a window in an Edinburgh apartment, a spy looks down on the street. Angry crowds have gathered, waving banners and chanting. It is 1706 and the protest is against the proposed Union with England.

The spy, an English writer called Daniel Defoe, sits down and writes: 'For every Scot in favour, there is 99 against!'

The few Scots in favour are mainly powerful nobles who stand to benefit from the Union. They will later be condemned as 'a parcel of rogues' who want to sell Scotland's independence for their own personal gain.

A hostile takeover

In England, those for the Union say it will boost national security and ensure the Scots can't break the Union of the Crowns by choosing a different monarch. Those against say most Scots don't want it, therefore it won't work.

In Scotland, many see the Union as a hostile takeover by England. Others say Scotland has been bankrupted by the Darien disaster and bad harvests, and that the English are already blocking Scotland's trade with other countries. So there is no alternative but to accept.

CHANGE AND CONTINUITY

The Union is reluctantly agreed, and on 1 May, 1707, it comes into effect. Scotland's parliament is closed and England's parliament becomes the British parliament of the United Kingdom – ruling Scotland, England and Wales.

Scottish ships become British ships and are allowed to trade freely, while Scots who produce grain and salt gain benefits. Scotland's churches, law courts and schools remain independent.

I PROMISE TO PAY THE BEARER

TANTO UBERIOR

Banking on it

A huge sum of money – £398,000 – known as 'the Equivalent' is paid out to sweeten the Union deal. This is to compensate the Scots for taking on a share of England's national debt – and for the failure of Darien.

The money is paid out by an organisation that later becomes the Royal Bank of Scotland. This follows the founding, in 1695, of the Bank of Scotland – the first bank in Europe to issue its own banknotes.

MASSACRE IN GLENCOE

It is February 1692 and in a cottage in the snowy mountain valley of Glencoe, Alastair MacIain, clan chief of the MacDonalds of Glencoe, awakes with a start. The door has been broken down by the men of clan Campbell who have been living in his village as guests for the past two weeks.

MacIain is stabbed to death while three dozen of his clansmen are put to the sword or shot.

As the Campbells set fire to houses, women and old people try to carry weeping children to safety. But the snow is deep and around forty more adults and youngsters die of exposure on the mountainsides.

Why the slaughter? The MacDonalds are Jacobites – this means they are loyal to King James, who was recently banished.

The new king, William of Orange, set a deadline for all Jacobite clan chiefs to swear allegiance to him. But Alastair of Glencoe failed to do so in time.

As a result, the Campbells, loyal servants of William, have been sent to punish their old clan rivals on his behalf. They arrive in Glencoe as friends, biding their time, before moving in for the kill.

JACOBITES

THE STUART CAUSE

The Massacre of Glencoe is part of a bigger story, which runs from 1688 to 1746 – the story of Jacobitism.

The word Jacobite come from *Jacobus*, the Latin word for James. The other name for Jacobitism is the Stuart Cause, which comes from the fact that King James is head of the originally Scottish royal family, the Stuarts.

All the British kings since the Union of the Crowns have been Stuarts. As with James VI, who became England's James I in 1603, two numbers are used for James VII – because he's also James II of England.

Jacobitism begins when the unpopular James VII and II is forced to give up his crowns and leave London in the winter of 1688–9.

James VII and II is exiled and some unfortunate Jacobites such as the MacDonalds are punished by the new King William.

The 1715 Uprising

The Jacobites stage several uprisings to try to restore the Stuarts, the biggest being in 1715. An unpopular new monarch, George of Hanover, has just been crowned and the Jacobites seize the opportunity.

But their army of 12,000 fails to defeat a mere 4,000 of King George's men at the Battle of Sheriffmuir, near Dunblane, and the uprising falls apart.

BONNIE PRINCE

THE LAST UPRISING

A prince born in Rome voyages to the remote north-western corner of the British Isles in 1745 to begin a rebellion. He is Prince Charles Edward Stuart – Bonnie Prince Charlie – a Jacobite royal determined to restore his family to the throne.

The Prince advances from the Western Isles to Glenfinnan in the Highlands, where Jacobite clansmen flock to join him. The determined, intelligent and handsome

Charlie then marches south alongside his men as bagpipers play along.

Joined by Lowland recruits, the Jacobites take Edinburgh and rout a government army at nearby Prestonpans. They then march into England and almost reach London before

CHARLIE

it all goes wrong.

Promised French reinforcements have not arrived and strengthened government forces are closing fast. As doubt sets in, a retreat is ordered.

Charlie's men are pursued back to the Highlands where a showdown takes place at the Battle of Culloden near Inverness.

Culloden is a defeat with dreadful consequences.

Victorious government commanders earn nicknames like 'Butcher' Cumberland and 'Hangman' Hawley by burning, torturing and executing their way through the glens.

The golfing soldier

A doctor, John Rattray, accompanies Prince Charlie on his campaign. Rattray is also winner of the first Scottish Open golf tournament, held in 1744, and a member of the Honourable Company of Edinburgh Golfers. This league of sporting gentlemen draws up the earliest surviving rules of the game.

OVER THE SEA WITH FLORA

After Culloden, Charlie flees back to the Western Isles. Hunted by the Royal Navy, he hides in caves and cottages on South Uist and Benbecula, where he meets a young Jacobite named Flora MacDonald.

Disguised as Flora's maid, the Prince travels over the sea to Skye then escapes to France, never to return. The Stuart cause is finished.

Why does Charlie lose Culloden?

At lunchtime on a cold 16 April, 1746, a Jacobite army of fewer than 7,000 men begins charging with claymores drawn across Culloden Moor under enemy artillery fire. The ground is boggy and the order to advance has not reached everyone, so the charge is chaotic.

This makes it easy for the 9,000-strong government force of English and Scots, including Highlanders, to shoot or cut down Jacobites from the sides, or flanks. In one bloody hour, the Jacobites are crushed.

TOBACCO LORDS

The final Jacobite defeat at Culloden was bloody, but some good comes of it. People are now able to go about their business more peacefully and the English are no longer worried about a dangerous rebellion spreading from Scotland.

This allows the tension and mistrust that has lingered between the two nations since the Union of 1707 to give way to a friendlier spirit of co-operation. And the Scots can finally reap the Union's rewards, by helping the English build the British Empire.

The most impressive early sign of Scotland's participation in Britain's overseas empire is the tobacco trade. Tobacco is grown on plantations in British colonies in America and the Caribbean, and sold to Europeans eager to smoke it. In the 1740s, just as the Jacobites are crushed, Scotland's share in this lucrative trade suddenly grows much bigger.

The key to this success is Glasgow. The city's location on Scotland's Atlantic coast, where the ocean's trade winds are most favourable, means that ships carrying tobacco and other American colonial produce can arrive up to three weeks faster than at other ports. The tobacco is then processed and shipped onward for sale across Britain and the continent.

This trade makes many Glasgow merchants spectacularly rich. They become known as 'the Tobacco Lords' and, as the city turns into a hive of commercial activity, new streets are named in honour of the most successful ones.

EMPIRE

Slave trade

In the 1760s you board a British ship, with several Scots among the crew, sailing south to Africa. The cargo includes cloth, machine parts and weapons made in Scottish factories.

When the ship arrives the cargo is traded for slaves – black Africans who are forced into the cramped lower decks to be transported west across the Atlantic to the Caribbean. Many slaves do not survive the long journey because of mistreatment, disease and malnutrition.

When the slave ships arrive, the survivors are forced to work on plantations often owned by Scots. Crops such as sugar, rum, molasses (a kind of sugar), hemp and cotton are then shipped back to Britain – along with tobacco bound for Glasgow.

Scots in India

Besides America and Africa, the British Empire also extends to India. By the 1800s a huge number of Scots work for the British East India Company, importing goods such as tea into Scotland.

Dundee, in particular, does well by importing an Indian vegetable fibre called jute, which is then manufactured into twine, sacks and carpets.

In the late 1700s, Scotland's success in the British Empire sparks a revolution. The colonial trade has brought in money and created huge demand for products. To meet this demand, money is invested in new Scottish factories producing everything from cloth to cannonballs on an industrial – vast – scale.

As more factories are built, more workers are needed for operating machines and other jobs. Scots begin leaving their villages in droves to work in city factories. This dramatic development, happening across Britain, is the Industrial Revolution.

STEAM POWER

The most important machine of the Industrial Revolution is a Scottish invention. To find it, we must stop off in the grounds of a stately home near Falkirk in the 1760s.

By a ravine containing a fast-flowing stream you notice a cloud of water vapour swirling among the trees. This steam leads to a small cottage connected by pipes to a large metal tank. Through the window you see a man working at a contraption made of cylinders, pistons and valves.

His name is James Watt. Born in Greenock in 1736 and employed at the University of Glasgow as a

scientific-instrument maker, here at Kinneil estate he is inventing an experimental condensing steam engine.

Unlike earlier steam engines, which work poorly, Watt's invention, once perfected, works brilliantly. And unlike water wheels that must be installed next to rivers to make power for factories, Watt's engine can be used anywhere.

During the next century and beyond, Watt's engine will pump floodwater from underground mines, allowing more coal to be cut to power yet more steam engines. These will then power machinery in countless factories, and propel a seemingly endless procession of steam ships and locomotives all over the world.

The farming revolution

Although many people are leaving villages for city factories, by the 1770s Scotland remains a very agricultural – or farming – nation. Yet, the Industrial Revolution happens on farms too.

Inventor James Small has come up with the iron 'swing plough', which works more effectively than old ploughs. This ground-breaking invention makes it easier to cultivate more crops to feed factory workers in the expanding cities.

The industrial kilt

Even in a remote Lochaber forest, the Industrial Revolution goes on. Workers here fell trees to make charcoal in order to smelt iron, which will be formed into machine components.

In the 1720s the men's big kilts, an ancient design, were shortened to make them more suited to industrial work. Soon all modern kilts become short.

PEOPLE OF GENIUS

As you have seen, by the late 18th century Scotland has become much wealthier than before thanks to two things: trade with the British Empire and the Industrial Revolution. The population is also growing.

One group of Scots is fascinated by this change in the nation's fortunes and they begin examining its causes and effects. They also think about where greater progress could lead in future.

This group has something else in common – they are all geniuses. The emergence of so many geniuses all at once might be down to the Union with England. As the nation is now ruled from London, Scotland's greatest talents – such as philosopher David

Wealth of Nations

Adam Smith is a brilliant Scottish Enlightenment economist from Kirkcaldy who lectures at Edinburgh and Glasgow universities. In 1776 he writes *The Wealth of Nations*, a book inspired by the Industrial Revolution and the British Empire.

Smith writes that when people strive to get the best deal for themselves, they are guided by an 'invisible hand' to also create benefits for others.

ENLIGHTENMENT

Hume – don't need to spend their time running a government.

Instead, they apply themselves to further improving not only their own country, but countries around the world. To do so, they must understand how the world works by solving its mysteries and discovering its secrets.

Scotland's talents come together at the nation's universities – especially Aberdeen, Glasgow and Edinburgh. They also meet in clubs and coffee houses to share new ideas and new discoveries, and debate new ways of doing things.

These people include, scientists, economists, engineers, lawyers, writers and historians. In fact, most are a combination of these things. Their collective genius is known as the Scottish Enlightenment.

The sky's the limit

'Look – the flying machine!' shouts a well-dressed gentleman. A vast globe filled with hot air, with a basket underneath containing the balloonist, is gliding over Edinburgh.

It is August 1784 and the Scottish capital is witnessing Britain's first ever hot-air-balloon flight. Piloted by James Tytler, a Church minister's son from Angus, this amazing spectacle captures the age of Enlightenment, when anything seems possible.

Man of rock

It's 1788 and a boat is being rowed around a sliced-up jumble of rocks known as Siccar Point in Berwickshire. One of those aboard, a scientist from Edinburgh called James Hutton, explains that the rocks are formed by natural processes over millions of years.

Before this, people did not really understand how old the Earth is or how it was made. So Hutton has made a startling discovery.

HEAVEN-TAUGHT PLOUGHMAN

It's 1787 and in a tavern a man is scratching poetry onto a window-pane with a diamond-tipped pen. His name is Robert Burns. He's recently become a famous writer, and his life reveals a lot about the times in which he lives.

Burns was born on 25 January 1759 in the Ayrshire village of Alloway. As he grew up, besides getting a good education, he worked on the family farm. He learned songs from old farm hands and began writing poetry.

One of his best-loved poems – 'To a Mouse' – came to him after he accidentally wrecked one of these wee, sleekit beasties' nests with his plough. The poem suggests that the Industrial Revolution is destroying nature to make way for farms and factories, such as one Burns worked in for a while making linen.

When his poems are published in 1786, Burns finds fame but not fortune. He considers following other Scots to the West Indies, a part of the British Empire, to make a good living.

Instead Burns perseveres as a writer. He travels to Edinburgh and finds the Scottish Enlightenment still in full swing, with a spectacular New Town being built.

Because of his farming background, Burns gets the nickname 'Heaven-taught ploughman'. Wealthy Edinburgh residents are fascinated by him, yet look down on his humble roots.

BURNS

REVOLUTION IN THE AIR

The fact that rich, titled people – the aristocracy – enjoy far greater privileges than everyone else angers Burns. He becomes interested in the 1776 American Revolution and the 1789 French Revolution, where common people seem to get more power and freedom.

In the 1790s, while working as an exciseman, a job that requires him to chase smugglers and pirates, Burns reportedly confiscates some cannons. He sends these to the revolutionaries in France.

Burns also writes a song, 'A Man's A Man for A' That', calling for people to be judged by their talent and skill rather than money or social rank. Published around the time of Burns' early death in 1796, the song inspires future generations to fight for their rights.

Poem of passion

Burns is a romantic, which means he writes poetry to stir his readers' passions. An example is his great love poem, 'A Red, Red Rose'.

Tam O' Shanter

In one of Burns' verse stories a farmer called Tam O' Shanter spends the evening in a pub then sets off home on horseback. But when he runs into the Devil and a gang of witches in a graveyard, Tam must run for his life.

THREADS

NEW LANARK

In 1786, just as Robert Burns' star is rising, something equally special is happening by the waterfalls of the River Clyde. Here, a new factory is set to become as famous in the world of industry as Burns is in literature.

The factory is New Lanark and its handsome buildings symbolise an important thread of Scotland's history – the making of cloth, or textiles. But New Lanark's most celebrated aspect is neither its excellent cotton yarn nor its fine architecture.

Nor is the factory especially renowned for its advanced cotton-spinning machines, patented by English industrialist Richard Arkwright, and powered by water-wheels, which

New patterns

Besides New Lanark, other exciting developments happen in the textile industry. In Paisley, weavers make a cloth with a droplet-shaped vegetable pattern inspired by designs from British colonies in Persia and India. It's known as Paisley Pattern. And in the Borders, a new woollen check called Tweed becomes fashionable.

harness the River Clyde. New Lanark's greatness rests on something much more important – the way its workers are treated.

Working conditions at New Lanark, where families live in high quality homes, are far better than those of most people during the Industrial Revolution. The factory has been set up by David Dale, a linen manufacturer and financier from Glasgow, who worked with Arkwright before going it alone.

Dale builds a school at New Lanark which, by 1796, has 510 pupils and 18 teachers. Yet despite this, life for the mill's children, who must work from the age of six, is still hard. Soon, however, a young man appears who will change all that.

ROBERT OWEN

When David Dale's daughter Caroline falls in love with Welshman Robert Owen, a Manchester mill manager visiting Scotland on business, they get married. Owen buys New Lanark in 1799, intent on improving workers' lives further.

The minimum age of millworkers is raised to 12 and the world's first crèche is set up. Now mothers can work while their infants are looked after.

In the early 1800s, Owen expands the school, ensuring children are taught music, literature and science. He rewards workers for doing well instead of punishing their mistakes. He also sets up a village shop selling goods to workers at low prices.

On the illustration:
WAVERLEY
IVANHOE
ROB ROY

WRITER AND PATRIOT

With his Tweed suit and walking stick, Walter Scott strides across early19th century Scotland like a giant. At least, his reputation does.

Born in Edinburgh in 1771, and raised there and in the Borders in a farming family, there's nothing remarkable about Scott's background or his career as a lawyer. But he's also a famous novelist and poet, greatly influenced by Robert Burns, whom he met in Edinburgh as a teenager.

Like Burns, Scott is a patriot, and tirelessly promotes Scotland with enormous energy. He publishes poems and novels celebrating the nation's history, such as *The Lay of the Last Minstrel*, *Rob Roy* and *Waverley*, to great success.

Then, in 1822, Scott organises a state visit of King George IV to Edinburgh. This is the first time a reigning British king or queen has set foot in Scotland since long before the Union of 1707.

Scott arranges for the king and Scottish nobles to take part in a magnificent pageant dressed in kilts and tartans. It's a bold celebration of the nation's culture, particularly the Highlands, which until then was still distrusted by many English as the home of rebellious Jacobites and a place best avoided.

SCOTT

WELCOME TO SCOTT-LAND

Scott's royal pageant of 1822 is like a huge advertisement that Scotland is now an inviting and attractive place. Of course, a few curious Englishmen have already toured the country, such as the

famously grumpy writer Samuel Johnson and his Scottish companion James Boswell.

But the high-profile visit of George IV encourages visitors to follow in a huge, unstoppable wave. This is the beginning of the modern Scottish tourist industry, as hotels spring up everywhere to accommodate people.

By enticing people to holiday north of the border, the tourism industry doesn't just make a lot of money. It helps conserve Scotland's national identity while strengthening the United Kingdom – just as Scott intended.

Solver of mysteries

It is 1818 and in a strongroom of Edinburgh Castle, Walter Scott looks on as chisels and hammers are used to break open an oak chest. Inside it, wrapped in linen cloths, are a crown, sword and sceptre – the Honours of Scotland.

These are the nation's crown jewels, which for more than a hundred years were believed lost. Thanks to Scott, who obtained royal permission to conduct a search, they have been found.

FOOD AND DRINK

In the 1820s, Scotland's population is more than 2 million – double what it was a hundred years before. This huge increase is mainly thanks to the know-how of the Industrial Revolution being put to work in the fields, helping farmers to grow plenty of crops which give people a healthy diet.

More people means a bigger market for products, and one of the most popular in Scotland's expanding towns is whisky. Millions of gallons are drunk every year and the quantity keeps rising fast.

Whisky is a strong alcoholic drink made from barley, and it's been made in Scotland for hundreds, if not thousands, of years. But in the past it has mostly been produced illegally.

The reason people make whisky illegally is this: if they came clean about what they were doing, they would have to pay a high excise duty – or tax – and

INDUSTRY

most would go out of business. So instead, whisky is made in secret and sold by smugglers.

In 1823, to try to get whisky makers to pay their taxes, the government reduces the duty so that it becomes much cheaper to make and sell whisky legally. The illegal distilleries are quickly replaced with legitimate businesses.

Using the latest technology to increase production, the modern 'Scotch whisky' industry is born. Whisky becomes very important to the economy, and plays a key role in people's social lives. The downside is that drunkenness becomes a serious problem, and during the 1800s there are campaigns to try to get people to drink less, or not at all.

Making malt whisky

Barley is ground then mixed with hot water, creating a sugary liquid. Yeast is added before the liquid is heated again and distilled to purify and strengthen it. Then it's kept in a cask for at least ten years, before being transported by ponies to market.

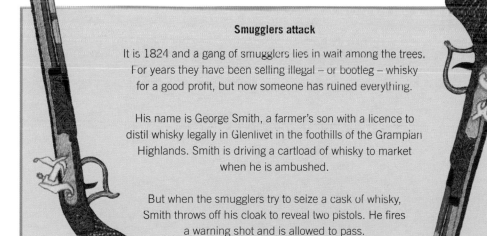

Smugglers attack

It is 1824 and a gang of smugglers lies in wait among the trees. For years they have been selling illegal – or bootleg – whisky for a good profit, but now someone has ruined everything.

His name is George Smith, a farmer's son with a licence to distil whisky legally in Glenlivet in the foothills of the Grampian Highlands. Smith is driving a cartload of whisky to market when he is ambushed.

But when the smugglers try to seize a cask of whisky, Smith throws off his cloak to reveal two pistols. He fires a warning shot and is allowed to pass.

THE IRISH

AN GORTA MOR

THE SEARCH FOR WORK

In Scotland's early 19th-century whisky bars, Irish voices stand out from the crowd. The Irish have come to this country in search of jobs. The work they find is hard, frequently dangerous, and a drink of whisky is often their only comfort.

Ireland formally joined the United Kingdom in 1801, but its people have not reaped the benefits of empire or the Industrial Revolution as the Scots have. While many bosses and landowners have become wealthy, most Irish people live in poverty.

To improve their life, many cross the Irish Sea to Scotland – or England – for work. They are often employed on very low wages as farm hands at harvest time, or as labourers known as navigators or 'navvies'.

Irish navvies provide the muscle for great Scottish engineering projects. They lay roads, build bridges and dig canals, so that Scotland's trade and economy can further improve.

At first, most Irish workers don't settle here. They go back to Ireland when their job is done, ready to return at the next opportunity.

This situation changes dramatically in the mid-1840s, when the potato crop fails in Ireland. The potato is people's main food, and without it they starve unless they can escape. A huge number leave, never to return, and many make Scotland their new home.

Medicine and murder

It's 1828 and in a packed medical lecture theatre in Edinburgh, the story of Irish immigration is taking a dark and deadly turn. A dead woman is laid before the assembled students, ready to be cut up, or dissected, so the students can learn about how the human body works.

But the person on the table did not die naturally. She was murdered, and her killers were paid in cash for her corpse. Her name was Mary Paterson and she, along with a boy called Daft Jamie and fourteen others, is a victim of William Burke and William Hare.

Burke and Hare are Irish navvies who have turned to crime. Burke's job is to lure victims to his lodgings, where he gets them drunk and suffocates them. The bodies are then sold for cash to Dr Robert Knox, who dissects them in the lecture theatre at Edinburgh University.

Hare is Burke's accomplice. When their crimes are discovered, Hare testifies against Burke at the trial to save his own skin. Burke is found guilty, executed and his body publicly dissected.

Union Canal

Burke and Hare helped build the Union Canal. It linked Edinburgh to Glasgow – via Falkirk and the earlier Forth–Clyde Canal – in time for George IV's royal visit in 1822.

READ ALL ABOUT IT

It is 31 January, 1829, and at an Edinburgh news-stand you pick up a copy of *The Scotsman* newspaper. Its journalists have written shocking eyewitness reports of the execution of notorious murderer William Burke, an event witnessed by celebrities such as novelist Walter Scott, a few days earlier.

The Scotsman started publication only a dozen years before, in 1817, but already it has gained a reputation for informing its readers of what's going on in Scotland's capital, the wider country and the world at large. Founded by lawyer William Ritchie and customs official Charles Maclaren, the newspaper vows to report with 'impartiality, firmness and independence'.

Newspapers are a key part of life in 19th-century Scotland. During this time, many more people than ever before become literate – able to read (and write) – thanks to improvements in education. Indeed, newspapers

NEWSPAPERS

themselves help improve people's reading skills.

The fast-growing populations of industrial towns and cities make it easy to sell newspapers to a lot of people, and to catch their interest by focusing on things affecting their local area. As a result, the market for news greatly increases.

Like other big industries springing up around this time, the newspaper business creates more jobs. Every time a giant newspaper printing press springs to life, causing the building around it to shake, a whole army of people is involved in making the end product – from reporters, editors and typesetters to ink suppliers, paper-mill workers and newsagents.

VOICES OF THE NATION

The Scotsman is far from being the first Scottish newspaper on the market. Through in Glasgow, the newspaper eventually known as *The Herald* has been in print since 1783.

Much older titles include the *Mercurius Caledonius*, printed between 1660 and 1661 and reappearing as *The Caledonian Mercury* in 1720. *The Scots Magazine* was founded in 1739 and Aberdeen's *Press and Journal* in 1747. Others are much younger: *The Oban Times* appears in 1861 and the *Daily Record* in 1895.

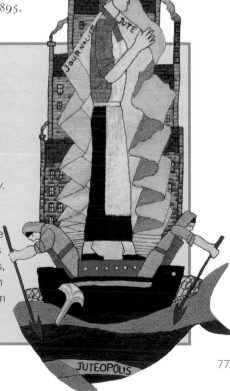

Jute, jam and journalism

The Dundee Courier is established in 1801 and journalism becomes an important business in the city, which later produces such famous comics as *The Beano* and *The Dandy*.

Dundee also becomes known for the manufacture of jam and marmalade, as well as materials, or textiles, made of jute. People begin calling it the city of jute, jam and journalism.

TRAVEL AND

THE RAILWAY AGE

In the 19th century people are brought together quicker than ever before thanks to amazing new methods of transport and communication, ranging from bicycles to telephones. Above all, probably the most important invention of this century is the steam train.

In 1842 you enter Edinburgh's new Haymarket Station and board the train for Queen Street in Glasgow. With a shunt-shunt noise the carriage moves off, and you settle down to read a newspaper article about the new 'railway age'.

Scotland's first railway was built in 1722 but it used horses to haul coal waggons along its wooden rails. Thanks to the work of inventors such as Scotland's James Watt and William Murdoch, horses were replaced by steam-powered engines, called locomotives, from 1817 onwards.

Since the 1830s, passenger trains have been connecting the corners of Britain. The Edinburgh–Glasgow line of 1842 is followed by a Scotland–England link in 1848.

By the middle of the century around 100,000 Scots work for railway companies and, for a while,

COMMUNICATION

almost a quarter of the world's steam locomotives are built in Glasgow.

Amazing new structures are built for railways. These include the arched stone viaduct soaring 30 metres above Glenfinnan and the 104-metre-high Forth Bridge. Designed by Scottish engineer William Arrol, the latter becomes a marvel of the industrial world when it is built to cross the River Forth between Edinburgh and Fife in 1890.

Thanks to train travel, everything from pears to postcards to people can be quickly transported for many miles. This changes the Scots' eating habits, the things they buy, how they work and where they go on holiday.

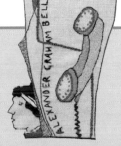

The telephone

On 10 March, 1876, in the American city of Boston, a Scotsman called Alexander Graham Bell speaks into a hand-held device. 'Mr Watson,' he says, 'come here – I want to see you.'

Bell's words zoom along an electric wire and are turned back into sound by a device held to the ear of Thomas Watson, Bell's assistant, in another room. Behold the telephone, Bell's amazing invention.

The pedal bicycle

'Look out!' shouts a man as he clatters past on a wooden contraption with iron-rimmed wheels. It is 1839 and on a lane near Dumfries you have almost been run over by blacksmith Kirkpatrick Macmillan.

He is testing a prototype of his new invention, the pedal bicycle. The pedals are connected to the back wheels by rods, allowing the rider to propel the bike forward.

ACTS OF REFORM

As the 1800s progress, the people of Scotland's growing cities demand a bigger say in how the country is run. This results in changes to the voting system, the laws affecting workers and other areas of life.

Until now, the country has been ruled by rich landowners, whose tradi-tional power and influence is in farming areas, not cities. But in 1832 the first Scottish Reform Act is passed. It massively increases the number of Scots who

Living underground

It Is 1840 and you are in a dark coal mine. Breathing is difficult; floodwater is at your knees. A girl carries a huge load of coal on her back.

'My name's Agnes Moffat,' she says. 'Father makes me work here and he gets my wages. I work fourteen hours a day and I've damaged my shoulder.'

When the public discover how bad things are in the mines, there is an outcry. In 1842 the law is changed: no women or boys under ten will work underground again.

THE PEOPLE

are allowed to vote in British elections – which decide who will form the next government – from 4,239 to more than 65,000.

The great industrial city of Glasgow is allowed to elect more Members of Parliament, or MPs, while the growing cities of Aberdeen, Dundee and Perth are allowed to elect MPs for the first time.

But the electoral system is still far from perfect because voting remains restricted to wealthy men. Most people are unable to vote until the law is changed by further acts in 1867, 1884 and the early 20th century.

From here on, political parties such as the Liberals and the Conservatives must try to win elections by appealing to a much wider range of people.

Ever since Robert Burns' time, people have been wanting greater political rights. The voting reforms reflect a general mood that power must be taken out of wealthy landowners' hands, and that better living and working conditions for people in overcrowded and dirty cities must be given a higher priority by the government.

The Great Disruption

It is 1843 and in a grand church in Edinburgh's New Town, almost two hundred people are staging a walk-out led by a preacher and economist called Thomas Chalmers. They are protesting at the fact Church ministers are being chosen by wealthy landowners, rather than by the congregation.

Chalmers and his rebels are soon joined by others. Calling themselves the Free Church of Scotland, they build new churches of their own.

MONARCH OF THE GLEN

The Victorian age is another name for 19th-century Britain, since Queen Victoria lives through most of it. As monarch, Victoria plays her part in enormous changes to British life – changes which at times are fast, furious and even frightening.

The Queen therefore seeks refuge in a peaceful place where, for her anyway, time stands still. That place is Highland Scotland.

In 1856, far away from the government in London, and far from the smoking factories and noisy cities, a train threads through the quiet wooded hills and moors of Deeside. It's the Royal Train and its passengers' destination is Balmoral Castle.

Balmoral is the new Scottish holiday home of Victoria and her husband

SCOTLAND

Prince Albert. It's been built to replace an older castle which the royals began renting in 1848 and bought in 1852, along with its vast hunting and fishing grounds.

Beginning her reign as a teenager in 1837, Victoria first visited Scotland with Albert in 1842 – two decades after Walter Scott organised the celebrated royal visit of her uncle, George IV. In fact, Scott is one of Victoria's favourite authors and his writings about Scotland are what first attracted her to the Highlands.

During long annual holidays at Balmoral, often during late summer when the heather is in bloom, Victoria keeps a diary of her Highland life with Albert,

their nine children, many servants and occasional guests – including the Prime Ministers of the day.

After Albert's death in 1861, the Queen's trusted Highland servant, John Brown, eventually persuades her to publish the diary as a way of getting over her grief. The book is a bestseller and makes people even more fascinated with the Highlands.

The royals' Balmoral life of hunting, fishing and wearing tartan encourages many English and Lowland Scottish city-dwellers to take the train north in search of fresh air and beautiful Highland scenery.

Local aristocrats accommodate the wealthiest guests in luxurious new castles and lochside hunting lodges, which are often built to look like Balmoral.

Birth of progress

Queen Victoria's Scottish connection doesn't stop at Balmoral. In 1853 she gives birth to one of her children, but the experience is much less agonising than it has been for women in the past thanks to a Scottish invention called anaesthesia.

Victoria has inhaled a drug called chloroform, the world's first usable anaesthetic, to reduce her pain. The man behind this breakthrough is a scientist from Bathgate called James Young Simpson.

THE CLEARANCES

While the royals enjoy an idyllic life at Balmoral, the Victorian age is a time of crisis for other people in Scotland's countryside. The crisis is largely caused by the actions of rich landowners. Their aim is to clear out tenant farmers and peasants to make way for larger farms which will return a bigger profit for the landowner.

Some families are thrown out and their houses burned down. But many choose to leave because life becomes just too hard – especially when there is a failure of the potato crop in the 1840s and people starve. The survivors leave in search of a better life in the city or overseas.

The worst clearances tend to be in the Highlands and Islands, and landowners such

Shearing sheep

It's springtime in the 1890s and a farmer in the Grampian Highlands is shearing a sheep. The wool or fleece will earn the farmer some money, but his life is hard and he's considering moving overseas.

THE LAND

as the Countess of Sutherland are notoriously cruel. But clearances have long gone on in the Lowlands, too.

When people move out, their land is often swallowed up by large farms. Deer parks are another popular money-spinner for Highland landowners, giving wealthy tourists a taste of the Queen's Highland life.

These visitors shoot stags – the 'monarchs of the glens' – in an empty landscape that was once home to most of Scotland's population.

Battle of the Braes

In 1882, in the village of Braes on the Isle of Skye, local tenant farmers known as crofters are told they must leave. Their landlord, Lord Macdonald, wants to give their land to bigger farms that will make him richer.

When 50 policemen are brought in from Glasgow to try to force people out, a battle erupts. Prisoners are taken away and sent to jail without a fair trial.

After another disturbance on the island results in more imprisonments, public sympathy leads to a change in the law: no longer can crofters in the west Highlands and Islands be evicted.

Carrying peats

In some places, life on the land continues much as before. It's 1902, a year after Victoria's death, and at Isbister in the Shetland Isles, two sisters haul heavy baskets or creels of peat on their backs for the fire. Knitting and chatting in the Shetlandic langauge as they go, the sisters still live a rural life far from the big cities.

SHIPBUILDERS

The Victorian age brings great change to life at sea as well as on land. There's a huge increase in the number of fishing, whaling, trade, travel and other ships in Scottish waters – and many are bigger and faster than ever before.

Thanks to the tools of the Industrial Revolution, the money made in the British Empire, and the arrival of steam power and metal-hulled ships – yet another Scottish invention – the nation's ship-builders become by far the best and most productive in the world.

The heart of Scotland's ship-building industry is the River Clyde. Colossal cranes tower over the hulking, half-built hulls of hundreds of ships in riverside yards from Glasgow to Greenock. To fit out the completed vessels with everything from steam engines to seat covers there are many other factories.

Clydeside is the workshop of the world, with hundreds of thousands of busy workers. The sight and smell of oils, chemicals, rubber, metals, fabrics and wood being poured, mixed, cut, crushed, sewn, forged, hammered, riveted, welded and burned is intoxicating – and the noise deafening.

Many Clyde-built ships are put to work in Scottish ports, but most are sold elsewhere. In the decade or

THE SEA

so after Queen Victoria's death, a fifth of all the ships on Earth are built in the yards of this single Scottish river.

But Scottish shipbuilding isn't confined to the Clyde. On the rivers Tay and Forth, and elsewhere, ships are turned out in huge numbers. It all adds up to an amazing national achievement.

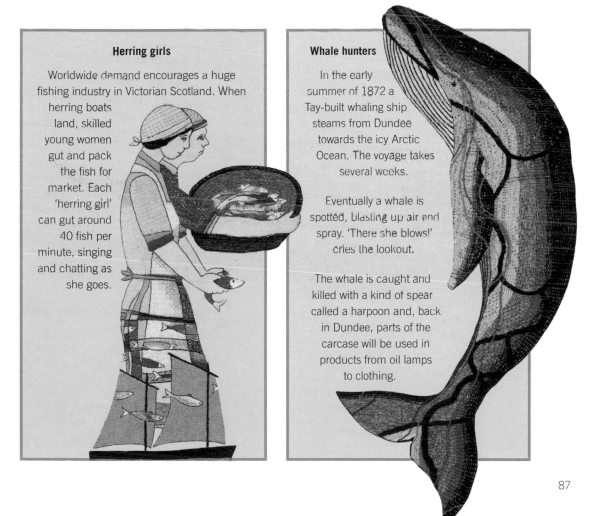

Herring girls

Worldwide demand encourages a huge fishing industry in Victorian Scotland. When herring boats land, skilled young women gut and pack the fish for market. Each 'herring girl' can gut around 40 fish per minute, singing and chatting as she goes.

Whale hunters

In the early summer of 1872 a Tay-built whaling ship steams from Dundee towards the icy Arctic Ocean. The voyage takes several weeks.

Eventually a whale is spotted, blasting up air and spray. 'There she blows!' cries the lookout.

The whale is caught and killed with a kind of spear called a harpoon and, back in Dundee, parts of the carcase will be used in products from oil lamps to clothing.

EXPLORING A CONTINENT

During Victorian times the British Empire grows to 14 million square miles and swallows up a quarter of the world's population – many of whom are unfairly exploited. Among the people responsible for this spectacular growth are Scottish explorers.

Africa is where many Scots explorers make their names, and among the most famous is David Livingstone. Born in 1813 in Blantyre near Glasgow, Livingstone works in a cotton mill before training as a doctor and Christian missionary, and then setting off on expeditions.

In the 1850s Livingstone travels along the mighty Zambezi River, charting huge areas of Africa never before visited by Europeans. He discovers a great waterfall which he names Victoria Falls in honour of the Queen.

After a second expedition, Livingstone sets off a third time in 1866 to find the source of the River Nile, but loses his way and is thought to have died.

Then, in November 1871, near the shores of Lake Tanganyika in central Africa, Livingstone is discovered by a Welsh journalist, who has trekked for hundreds of miles through the jungle to find him.

'Dr Livingstone, I presume?' says the journalist, Henry Morton Stanley.

With Stanley's aid, Livingstone continues trying to track the Nile until he dies in what is now Zambia in May 1873.

AFRICA

SAVING CHILDREN

David Livingstone's story inspires Mary Slessor – a jute worker from Dundee – to go to Africa. In the 1880s she works in Calabar, Nigeria, living among the people while teaching Christianity and other European ideas.

Slessor discovers that many mothers in Calabar consider having twins to be an evil curse, and abandon the babies. Slessor takes such babies into care, and adopts one as her own daughter, Janie.

Facing death

Livingstone and Slessor both die of disease during African missions. But other Scots suffer worse fates.

In 1806 a scientist from Selkirk called Mungo Park is on the River Niger when his canoe gets stuck on a rock. Suddenly, a hail of spears is launched from the shore and Park is drowned trying to escape.

Twenty years later Alexander Gordon Laing, from Edinburgh, is the first European to reach Timbuktu by crossing the Sahara Desert. But upon leaving the fabled city he is ambushed by bandits and killed.

EDUCATION FOR ALL

You look through a window and see children reading words from their teacher's blackboard. This is a Victorian classroom and it shows that the dream of 16th-century Reformers has become reality. Every part of Scotland now has a school.

Thanks to schools in places like Caithness in the Highlands, three out of four pupils can read and write by the middle of the 19th century. These children are among the best educated in Europe.

But other parts of Scotland are not doing as well. Fewer than half the children in Lanarkshire, for example, attend lessons. And although more and more girls are going to school, they are less likely than boys to receive a good education.

Catholic children meanwhile often lose out because many come from poor Irish immigrant families. They must work rather than attend school to survive.

A big step forward is taken in 1872, when the

CLASSROOM

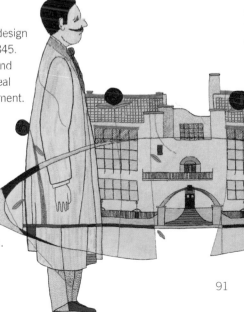

Education Act makes it compulsory for all children aged five to thirteen to go to school. This Act and others mean that the government – or state – takes full responsibility for educating the majority of Scottish children.

Very poor families are given some money so their children can go to school instead of having to work. Meanwhile the need for more teachers gives many women the opportunity to have a career, like men, for the first time.

In 1870 the Edinburgh Educational Institute For Girls is created. In fact, it's a new name for a girls' school that was founded back in 1694 by an enterprising widow called Mary Erskine.

One of the oldest girls' schools in the world, Mary Erskine's also becomes one of many private schools for the children of wealthy Scots.

Sign language

Some Victorian pupils are educated in sign language thanks to Thomas Braidwood, whose school for deaf and dumb children was the first in Britain.

When Braidwood set up his school in Edinburgh back in 1780, it tended to be only well-off people who could afford its fees. Eventually, though, all deaf and dumb children are taught sign language.

Art school

A college teaching art and design is founded in Glasgow in 1845. The city's industrial boom and variety of life make it the ideal place for such an establishment.

In 1897 work is begun on an amazing new building for what is now called the Glasgow School of Art. It's designed in a style called Art Nouveau by architect Charles Rennie Mackintosh.

Hill and Adamson

The first Scots ever to be photographed are Victorians, and many of them are snapped by David Hill and Robert Adamson. Their camera is a box on a tripod with a hole at the front for capturing light to make a photograph.

ELECTRICITY, LIGHT AND MAGIC

Heat, light and electricity are natural forces that shape the universe, but until the 19th century they are not properly understood. Two Victorian Scottish schoolboys help reveal how these apparently magical forces work, and how they can be used most effectively in gadgets from cameras to electric clocks and radios.

One of these boys is Alexander Bain, a bright crofter's son from Caithness. He lands a job as a watch-maker's apprentice in Wick before moving to Edinburgh, then London, where he attends lectures on the possible uses of electrical science.

In 1840, Bain uses his knowledge and skills to construct the world's first electric clock. Since there are no electrical sockets in

SCIENCE

ALEXANDER BAIN
ELECTRIC CLOCK

those days Bain also builds a battery, which takes electricity from metal plates buried in the ground.

While Bain is busy inventing, a lad called James Clerk Maxwell is being nicknamed 'dafty' by his classmates in Edinburgh. Little do they know he will become one of the world's greatest scientists.

In 1861 Maxwell thrills a scientific audience in London with the world's first colour photograph. He also makes them laugh with his Scottish sense of humour, since it's a picture of a tartan ribbon.

Maxwell reveals that physical forces we see and feel around us – like light, colour, heat, electricity and magnetism – are all part of a phenomenon known as the electromagnetic spectrum, which also includes radio waves and nuclear radiation.

Without these forces photographs would simply be blank, and later gadgets like radios and microwave ovens would not work. Maxwell's revelations are greatly admired by later scientists such as Albert Einstein.

Mary Somerville

A woman from Jedburgh called Mary Somerville finds that in the late 1700s and 1800s most people regard science as a subject only men should know about. Somerville disagrees. Encouraged by her uncle, she teaches herself with books and becomes a celebrated Victorian writer and astronomer.

Camera Obscura

In 1890s Edinburgh, at the top of a narrow spiral staircase, you find a dark room containing an amazing panoramic image of the city. It's known as the Camera Obscura and the image is created by daylight flooding in through a tiny hole.

LET THE GAMES BEGIN

During Victorian times, sport takes off as never before, particularly in the cities, where huge numbers of people live. Industrial skills are used to build playing fields and stadiums. Scotland and England play a joint role in creating modern rugby and football, but other sports are particular to Scotland. These include shinty, curling and Highland Games.

The royal interest in all things Highland plays a big part in the creation of Highland Games during the 1800s. These games bring together and update traditional sports for a programme of formal competitions held in the same place on the same date every year. They also have a Highland flavour, even if they are not actually staged in the Highlands.

The Braemar Gathering is the most well-known of these games. It was first held in 1832, at a time when Highland gatherings were springing up across Scotland, and in places such as North America where Scots emigrated because of the Clearances.

Queen Victoria becomes an enthusiastic patron of the Braemar Gathering. Events

SPORTS

Sticks and stones

Popular Victorian sports include curling, a game in which stones are glided across a frozen surface, and whose first formal rules are made in Edinburgh in 1838. Formal rules are made in 1893 for shinty, a ball game played with sticks and popular in the Highlands.

here and at other major games typically include strongman or 'heavy' events, such as tossing the caber – a tree trunk – in the air.

Another key ingredient is music and dance. Highland dancing is very athletic, and traditionally the competitions are for men – often soldiers, as are many players in bagpiping events.

On less peaceful occasions, the same men can be found piping Scottish army regiments into battle during Victorian wars to protect and expand the British Empire.

Football and rugby

Ball games have a very long history in Scotland, but the modern games of rugby and football – or fitba – appear during Victorian times. When factory workers get a little free time on a Sunday afternoon, for example, vast crowds of 100,000 or more pack stadiums to watch football.

The first ever international rugby match is held in Edinburgh in 1871. The teams are Scotland versus England, and the Scots win. The following year Scotland play England again in the first ever international football match. Associations for football and rugby are soon formed to organise matches between clubs within Scotland.

MASTER STORYTELLER

Rain drums on the window-panes of a house during the miserable Scottish summer of 1881. The writer Robert Louis Stevenson and his stepson, Lloyd, are at the fireside drawing a map of an imaginary 'treasure island'. It gives Stevenson an idea for a story.

Stevenson becomes one

of the world's great writers. Books such as *Treasure Island*, the adventure story inspired by the map and featuring the pirate Long John Silver, and *Dr Jekyll and Mr Hyde* – a chilling tale about a man with a good side and a wicked side – appear on bookshelves around the world.

Stevenson is born in Edinburgh in 1850. Determined to be an author, Stevenson does not become successful until he is in his mid-30s.

Like many Scots of industrial times, including writers Robert Burns and Walter Scott, Stevenson is crippled by illness. Though the Victorian age is full of marvels, medicine has not yet caught up with killer

diseases like tuberculosis – which makes Stevenson cough up blood.

Another shadow overhanging Stevenson is evil. Raised with very Scottish religious values, Stevenson learns that evil lurks within all of us and if we're not careful it will take control – as his character Dr Jekyll discovers.

STEVENSON

MAN OF THE WORLD

Stevenson writes many adventure stories to give his readers an escape from everyday city life and its troubles. But he too seeks an escape – from sickness.

In search of a healthier climate, Stevenson does what many Victorian Scots do: he goes abroad. After living in Switzerland, France, England and America he finally voyages to the South Pacific and settles with his wife and family in Samoa.

In 1894 the sickly Stevenson collapses and dies trying to open a bottle of wine. One of his last books is *The Ebb-Tide*, which criticises the way Europeans are colonising other parts of world. It is typical Stevenson: a brilliant story whose characters reach out and grab you.

Kidnapped

A gunshot rings out in the woods and a man on horseback falls to the ground. Colin Campbell of Glenure, a government land agent, has been murdered. But why? And by whom?

More than a century after this event in 1752, known as the 'Appin Murder', its unanswered questions inspire Stevenson. He transforms real life murder suspect Alan Breck Stewart into a fictional character in *Kidnapped*, a tale about a teenager's adventures in the Scottish Highlands.

CHARTING NEW LANDS

By the early 1900s – called the Edwardian age after King Edward VII – exploration is a Scottish speciality. Besides the Scots explorers of Africa, there are those who travel to the furthest corners of the earth in the Arctic and Antarctic, those who explore the Americas, and those who map parts of their own country.

The scientific charting of unknown lands begins at home, back in the 1740s. After the Jacobite defeat at Culloden, the government is determined to ensure any future uprisings are quickly found and crushed. For this they need accurate maps, but there is none available. So they make their own.

Surveyors, who study the landscape with special scientific instruments, are sent to the Highlands to make military maps known as the Ordnance Survey. Before long, other Scots grow eager to chart new lands overseas.

An outstanding Victorian explorer is Dr John Rae from Orkney. In the 1840s and 50s he goes on heroic expeditions to the Canadian Arctic, mapping huge areas previously unknown to outsiders.

Rae is respectful to the native Inuit people, who teach him how to survive the Arctic's deadly snowstorms and ice sheets. He discovers a valuable shipping route known as the Northwest Passage.

Rae is followed by another Scots surveyor of Canada called Sandford Fleming, inventor of the 24-hour clock.

Time seems to freeze at the opposite end of the world in 1902, when the Dundee-built ship *Discovery* is locked in the Antarctic ice

EXPLORERS

and doesn't move for two years. The *Discovery* carries the British National Antarctic Expedition, which maps some of the polar continent.

Another impressive undertaking happens at the same time: the Scottish National Antarctic Expedition. Led by William Speirs Bruce, it sets up the first Antarctic weather station, discovers unknown territory, and collects valuable animal, plant and mineral specimens.

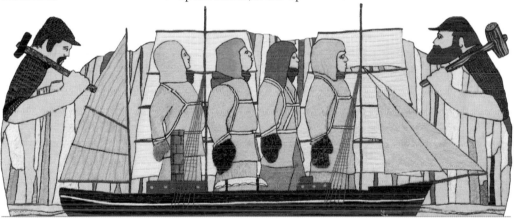

Mountain man

A bearded man in thick tweeds and stout boots is lashed by hailstones as he scrambles to a mountain summit. He is Sir Hugh Munro and he has just discovered another 'Munro' – a Scottish mountain over 3,000 feet high – to add to his list of Munros, published in 1891.

Grandfather of parks

John Muir is an explorer and preserver of native lands and wildernesses. A Scotsman who emigrates to America, Muir helps set up the Yosemite National Park in 1890 and it becomes the cornerstone of the American national parks system.

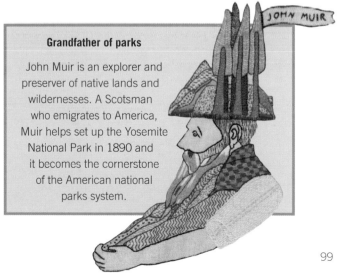

BATTLE COMMENCES

In 1914 the world goes to war, with Scots in the thick of it. The conflict has brewed for decades, as Britain and other European empires scrambled to dominate the world, fighting smaller wars in Africa, Asia and elsewhere.

Now, like giants squabbling over the last scrap of food, these empires must fight to the death. The result, thanks to awesomely destructive new weapons, is four years of terrible bloodshed.

Around 700,000 Scots join what becomes known as the First World War, or 'Great War', as Britain joins with other Allies – including France and Russia. Their enemy is the empires of Germany, Austro-Hungary, Ottoman Turkey and others.

In 1918 the Allies win, but at a massive cost. Austro-Hungary and Russia are torn apart; Britain and Germany exhausted. Millions die, including over 100,000 Scots. Some estimates reckon Scotland loses a bigger proportion of its population than any country apart from Turkey and Serbia.

WAR

FIGHTING SPIRIT

Scotland's contribution to Britain's war effort is distinctive. Kilted soldiers fight in Scottish regiments such as the Black Watch and Gordon Highlanders. And all Scots, whichever force they're in, are united by the nation's fighting spirit.

This spirit comes from a history of defending Scottish independence: the Caledonians who defeated Rome; Wallace and Bruce who defeated England; the Highland clans who fought for their way of life. It has been kept alive by Scottish regiments fighting for Britain in a series of Victorian wars, and now it motivates Scots to confront death again.

Many Scots fight on the Western Front – a battle line running from Belgium to Switzerland. Along this front, place-names such as Loos, the Somme and Ypres – a city that stages three Earth-shattering battles – become killing fields.

Soldiers shelter in trenches because the enemy firepower is too great for them to advance. Whenever they do, thousands are killed and often little ground is gained.

It is only when British commander Douglas Haig unleashes new fighting methods including the tank – an armoured vehicle that can move against heavy artillery – that Britain gains the upper hand. Haig, a whisky-maker's son from Edinburgh, firmly believes in the British Empire and Scotland's fighting spirit.

Sea and air power

Scotland has a key presence in the wartime navy and air force. David Henderson, a ship-builder's son from Glasgow, is the driving force behind the daredevil Royal Flying Corps. Meanwhile Scapa Flow, Orkney, is home to the British navy's Grand Fleet, which defeats Germany at the Battle of Jutland in 1916.

THE HOME

RAIDS AND RESISTANCE

Away from the front lines, the First World War deeply affects people back in Scotland on the 'home front'. Lives are lost in enemy air-raids and other disasters, families send letters and gifts to their men on the front, factory workers produce weapons, and a few bold voices criticise the conflict.

In the run-up to war there is an 'arms race' –

Cruel fate of heroes

People die on the home front as a result of German air-raids, such as the Zeppelin airship attack on Edinburgh in April 1916, but more are killed by military accidents.

On 22 May, 1915, on a railway line near Gretna close to the border with England, a train full of soldiers crashes into a parked train. A minute later a third train smashes into the wreckage, which catches fire.

Most of the 227 people killed are Royal Scots travelling to the war's Eastern Front. It is the worst railway disaster in British history.

Another catastrophe occurs before dawn on New Year's Day, 1919, when naval yacht HMV Iolaire strikes a reef at Stornoway harbour on the Isle of Lewis, and quickly sinks amid rough seas and a fierce gale.

The 280 sailors aboard had been looking forward to seeing their families again after surviving the war. But in their heavy uniforms and boots, most drown as they try to get away. Only 75 survive.

FRONT

a competition between countries to build the latest weaponry – which intensifies once hostilities break out. Scotland's factories make everything from bombs, bullets and battleships to soldiers' uniforms and bagpipes for regimental bands.

Outside the cities, sheep farms – many created by the Clearances   provide meat, milk and wool for the troops and uniform-makers, while other farms grow oats for soldiers' porridge. In farm–houses and city tenements, mothers read their sons' letters from the front lines and send boxes of sweets and magazines in return.

There are also those who oppose the war because they think it immoral. Some of these 'conscientious

Warhorses

Scottish farms supply some of the many horses used in the war. Most carry weapons and supplies, but others ride into battle in cavalry regiments such as the Royal Scots Greys.

objectors' are religious. Others such as Clydeside worker John MacLean are political.

MacLean is jailed for arguing that ordinary workers have nothing to gain by going to war except to be killed. Meanwhile English officer Siegfried Sassoon writes anti–war poetry while recuperating from battle at Craiglockhart Military Hospital, Edinburgh.

ELSIE INGLIS

The First World War marks a major development in Scotland's history, as women begin to gain freedom. The struggle for equal rights with men, sometimes known as the women's suffrage movement, began long before the war. But around this time it reaches its peak, with women taking part in the war and drawing attention to their cause.

One woman who stands out is Edinburgh doctor Elsie Inglis. One of the first women to qualify as a doctor in Britain, Inglis opens a hospital in Edinburgh to improve care for mothers and babies in 1894. When war is declared in 1914 she founds the Scottish Women's Military

Bomb-makers

On the home front, where weapons such as high-explosive shells and tanks are manufactured, the workers are often young women. It's dangerous work and the chemicals involved turn the women's skin yellow.

AT WAR

Hospitals. These are female-run medical units for treating wounded soldiers on the front lines, but their establishment is opposed by the men in government. On the Eastern Front, where regiments such as the Royal Scots fight in a part of Turkey called Gallipoli,

Inglis leads a unit that comes under enemy bombardment near the Black Sea. The unit retreats with the soldiers and continues treating wounded men.

The Scottish Women's Military Hospitals' success helps demonstrate that women deserve equal

rights. After Inglis dies of cancer in 1917, aged just 53, her work lives on, and in 1925 the Elsie Inglis Memorial Maternity Hospital is opened in Edinburgh.

The long struggle

Scottish women have been at war for a long time, not against an enemy army, but against the UK parliament because it denies them the right to vote in elections as men do.

The Scottish Women's Suffrage Federation appears in 1906, with Elsie Inglis among its founders. Some women take extreme actions to draw

JESSIE STEPHEN

attention to their cause, including pouring acid into post boxes, slashing royal portraits and burning public buildings – such as Ayr Racecourse and Leuchars Railway Station.

Militant suffragettes are sent to prison, where many go on hunger strike to gain publicity for the cause. Flora Drummond, a Scottish suffragette postmistress, is sent to prison at least nine times.

British victory in the war leads in 1918 to an extension of voting rights to all men, because the authorities fear revolution if it does not reward ordinary soldiers for risking their lives. But women's wartime heroism and the suffrage campaign also force the government to give some women the vote – later extended to all women.

PERTH PRISON

REVOLUTION IN THE AIR

Shortly after the First World War a crowd gathers on Clydeside to listen to a speech. The speaker says the government's promises to provide better houses and jobs for the war's survivors have been broken.

The man is a member of a political movement called Labour. Founded in late Victorian times, Labour encourages workers to join trade unions – groups that try to make factory bosses pay better wages by refusing to work if necessary, also known as going on strike.

Labour supporters are encouraged by two wartime events: the 1917 communist revolution in Russia, where workers' leaders take control of the government; and the 1918 British reform which gives the vote to working-class men – many of whom support Labour.

Central to the workers' struggle is the Labour Party. Created in 1906 to fight elections, the Labour Party is built on the foundations of earlier parties such as the original Scottish Labour Party.

The Labour Party's early leaders are Scots. Lanark-shire's Kier Hardie is the first Labour MP and Ramsay Macdonald the first Labour Prime Minister.

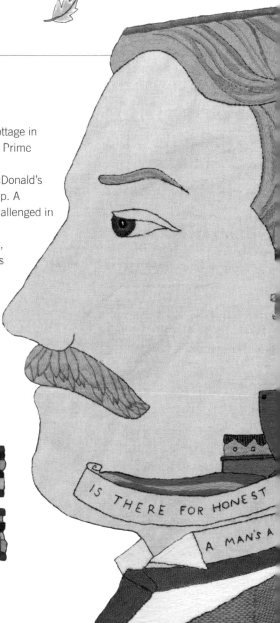

Ramsay MacDonald and the General Strike

Ramsay MacDonald, the son of a housemaid, is raised in a cottage in Lossiemouth, Morayshire. He rises to become the first Labour Prime Minister of Britain in 1924.

Undermined by newspapers owned by rich enemies, MacDonald's government soon collapses. But Labour radicals do not give up. A government of Conservatives, representing big business, is challenged in 1926 by a huge General Strike.

The General Strike might cause a Russian-style revolution, but its leaders lack a clear plan of action and MacDonald does not support it. Eventually the strike ends, at great personal cost to the workers who supported it.

In 1929, MacDonald is re-elected just as the world market collapses. A five-year Great Depression causes millions to lose their jobs.

To try to unite the country during the crisis MacDonald forms a National Government, but Labour expels him for working with Conservatives. The stress takes its toll on MacDonald, who dies aged 71 in 1937.

Tenement life

Neighbours share a toilet and large families are packed into too few rooms. But during the Great Depression of the 1930s, the slum tenement flats of Scotland's industrial cities have a strong community spirit and people help each other during hard times.

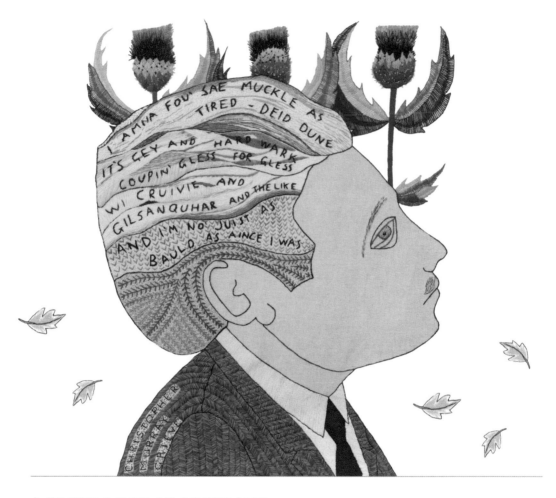

I AMNA FOU' SAE MUCKLE AS
TIRED - DEID DUNE
IT'S GEY AND HARD WARK
COUPIN' GLESS FOR GLESS
WI CRUIVIE AND
GILSANQUHAR AND THE LIKE
AND I'M NO JUIST AS
BAULD AS AINCE I WAS

CHRISTOPHER MURRAY GRIEVE

A FRESH LOOK AT SCOTLAND

A man lies on a hillside under the light of the moon and notices the jagged outline of a thistle – Scotland's national flower. Looking at the thistle makes him think about his nationality, the meaning of his life and many other things besides, in a famous 1926 poem by writer Hugh MacDiarmid.

MacDiarmid is a leader of what came to be known as the 'Scottish renaissance'. This is a period in the early 20th century when Scottish writing, art and music flourishes.

During this time writers try to reflect the fast and confusing changes going on in the world. Some aim to shape future events. And

RENAISSANCE

others prefer to offer readers an escape from such concerns. Writers Anna 'Nan' Shepherd and Lewis Grassic Gibbon, for example, tell stories about women living in Scottish villages and cities which are dramatically affected by the Industrial Revolution, the First World War and new political ideas.

Writers such as MacDiarmid aim to restore the Scots language, which has been neglected in favour of English since the Union. Others, such as poet Sorley MacLean, write in Gaelic, the original language of the Highlands and Islands.

Most importantly, Scottish renaissance writers let their imaginations run free. Novelist Naomi Mitchison includes fantasy and science fiction among her many books, while John Buchan's *The Thirty-Nine Steps* is an international spy thriller with a Scottish dimension.

Fantasy and comedy

A boy who can never grow up flies through the night air and hovers by an open window. Dressed in leaves and playing a flute, he has come to see a girl called Wendy. Peter takes Wendy and her brothers to the island of Neverland for a great big adventure.

Peter Pan is created by James Matthew Barrie from Kirriemuir, who writes about Peter's fantasy world between 1902 and 1911. Barrie is inspired by Scottish folklore and his hugely popular stories say a lot about human nature.

Another entertaining type of Scottish literature that emerges is comic strips. Desperate Dan, created in 1937 by D C Thompson publishers in Dundee, is a comic-book cowboy who sleeps in an old broken-down shack in Cactusville, Texas, and eats cow pies that make him incredibly strong.

Artists

As well as writers, the Scottish renaissance is about artists who tell stories with paint or other materials. In bright and thought-provoking artworks, painters such as Stanley Cursiter and JD Fergusson depict everything from human bodies to battleships and city streets.

SCOTLAND AND THE WAR

In 1939 another world war begins with Scotland again in the thick of it. Enemy attacks on Scotland bring death and destruction, as meanwhile many Scots sent to fight overseas are killed or taken prisoner.

The Second World War begins partly because Germany is very heavily punished for losing the First World War. Germans want revenge for this, and turn to the new Nazi Party of Adolf Hitler to provide it.

In the late 1930s the Nazis seize countries considered to be German property, such as Austria and Czechoslovakia. But when they invade Poland in 1939, it is obvious they aim to take over the whole of Europe.

On 3 September 1939, Britain declares war against Germany – and the enemy immediately attacks Scotland.

WORLD WAR

INTRUDER ALERT

Terror on Scotland's home front begins just hours after war is declared. The Clyde-built passenger ship *Athenia* is sunk by a German submarine near the Outer Hebrides while sailing from Glasgow to Canada.

It's the first British ship to be sunk in the war, and more than 100 people are killed. But there is much worse to come.

Around midnight on 14 October, another German submarine creeps into Scapa Flow, in Orkney, one of the bases used by Britain's Royal Navy. The intruder, *U-47*, spots Royal Navy battleship HMS *Royal Oak*.

U-47 fires underwater bombs called torpedoes, which strike the *Royal Oak*, causing the ship's ammunition stores to explode. She sinks in 13 minutes with the loss of 833 crew, many just teenagers.

Two days later, nine German fighter-bombers swoop on Rosyth naval base on the Forth, damaging three warships and killing 16 men.

But then comes a glimmer of hope. On 28 October, a German Heinkel 111 plane is attacked by RAF aircraft over East Lothian. The Heinkel crashes near the village of Humbie, and becomes the first enemy shot down during the war.

A noble sacrifice

As the German army advances across Europe, Britain sends troops to confront them. But no real action is taken until the Germans invade France in May 1940, and by then it's too late. The Germans are unstoppable and the British retreat.

The Scottish soldiers of the 51st Highland Division and a battalion of Royal Scots from the Lothians hold off the Germans so that other troops can escape from Dunkirk on the French coast back to Britain. Their bravery saves 340,000 soldiers, but more than 10,000 Scots are taken prisoner.

CRAMOND

THREAT OF INVASION

By midsummer 1940, central and western Europe is in the grip of Nazi Germany or its allies. Britain is left isolated and enters a frightening period sometimes called its 'darkest hour'.

While Germany's air force bombards England, confronting the RAF in the 'Battle of Britain', Scotland is attacked by aircraft from Nazi-occupied countries such as Denmark and Norway.

For hundreds of miles around Scotland's coast, defences of concrete blocks and machine-gun bunkers are built in case of a full-scale invasion launched from Norway.

Many Norwegians courageously resist the Nazis, and the Scots help them. Norwegian fighters are taken across the North Sea by a network of secret-service boats, called the 'Shetland Bus'. Trained in the Highlands, they return to Norway to carry out special attacks against the Germans called sabotage operations.

HOUR

The Clydebank Blitz

By 1941, the threat of invasion by the German army has receded, but air attacks are far from over. For many Scots the worst is still to come.

During two nights in March 1941, the Germans launch an air raid, or Blitzkrieg, against Clydebank. Blitzkrieg means 'lightning war' – attacking swiftly with overwhelming force – a tactic that has defeated other countries.

The target is the Clyde's great shipping and engineering works, and the families who live roundabout. Hundreds of aircraft drop more than 1,000 bombs, wrecking 8,500 homes and killing 528 people.

Germany is convinced Britain will surrender. On the night of 10 May, 1941, a Messerschmitt BF 110 flies over southern Scotland and its pilot parachutes to the ground. He is Rudolf Hess – deputy to Nazi leader Adolf Hitler – on a secret mission to try to negotiate a deal with Britain.

But British Prime Minister Winston Churchill refuses to back down. German attacks continue and, on 24 May, Clyde-built battlecruiser HMS *Hood* is sunk – taking 1,415 men down with her.

Dig for Victory

In spite of huge loss of life, Churchill's determination not to give in encourages the British people. They emerge from air-raid shelters dug in gardens and fields to rebuild factories and homes.

They also dig up lawns to plant vegetables, and make yards for pigs and chickens. This is the advice of the 'Dig for Victory' campaign of Professor John Raeburn from Aberdeen. The aim is for people to grow their own food rather than rely on scarce supplies.

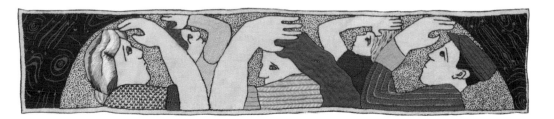

A NEW HOPE

In 1943, in a sandy field on the Aberdeenshire coast, you find evidence that the tide of war is turning in favour of Britain and its Allies. A new RAF airfield has been built here and its pilots are cheerful and optimistic.

They know Germany is in trouble. It has been heavily defeated in Russia and North Africa, its U-Boats are no longer masters of the sea, and the mighty United States of America has joined the Allied side.

By 1944, fully trained squadrons of fighter-bombers are taking off from aerodromes all over eastern Scotland. They attack German ships, cutting off vital supplies of iron ore and other materials the Nazis desperately need to make weapons.

Meanwhile, a vast army of Allied troops is assembled in Britain for a counter-attack to free Europe.

ON TO VICTORY

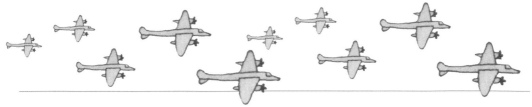

D-DAY

On 6 June 1944, special landing craft ram the beaches of Normandy on the French coast. Their ramps crash open and 150,000 soldiers come ashore under heavy machine gun fire. This is the great Allied counter-attack, known as D-Day. Among the huge number of Scottish soldiers taking part is a man on a special mission. Bill Millin, the only soldier in a kilt, spurs on elite troops called Commandos with tunes from his bagpipes.

D-Day is a spectacular success, but so too are other operations. In Italy, Scottish soldiers play a key role in bloody battles that root out Nazi forces. And Scots are among the international crews of RAF bombers which reduce German cities to rubble.

By summer 1945, Germany is defeated and the war is over. The Allies discover the remains of around 6 million people executed by the Nazis. This mass-murder is known as the Holocaust.

Who dares wins

Scotland's beaches, lochs and mountains provide a training ground for D-Day and other Allied operations. Commando brigades, for example, train in the Highlands to carry out daring raids behind enemy lines to speed up the Allied advance.

Inspired by the Commandos, Perthshire man David Stirling sets up the Special Air Service, or SAS, to sabotage German forces in North Africa. The SAS motto is 'Who dares wins'.

Prayers for peace

Imprisoned Italian soldiers are sent to Orkney to improve the defences at the naval base at Scapa Flow. They are also allowed to use scrap materials to transform a primitive prison hut into a beautiful chapel, where prayers for peace are said.

MODERN LIFE

From the ruins of war rises a new Scotland of concrete, plastic and hope. New homes are built, filled with amazing gadgets such as TVs and washing machines.

Travel becomes easier with affordable cars, better roads and planes. A free national health service is created to look after people.

But there are clouds on the horizon. The British Empire is collapsing, and the industries upon which Scotland depends face extinction.

Still, the post-war years begin optimistically. Between 1947 and 1966, five 'new towns' are built – East Kilbride, Glenrothes, Cumbernauld, Livingstone and Irvine. Instead of cramped city slums with shared toilets and little green space, families have modern homes with gardens.

And in the home, new appliances appear. The television was pioneered in the 1920s by Scottish inventor John Logie Baird. From the 1950s, TV sets begin popping up every-where.

WORLD

For many, the 'wireless' radio is more important than TV. Another Scotsman, John Reith, set up the British Broadcasting Corporation – the BBC – in 1923 to broadcast news and entertainment to radios and later TVs.

Another household gadget is the washing machine. Such devices make it easier for women to combine housework with paid jobs, although the washing machine actually puts many washer women out of a job.

Industrial ups and downs

Scotland's new towns turn out to be badly designed and poorly constructed. But a bigger problem affects the country – how to keep people working.

A high-tech coal mine intended to provide jobs in Glenrothes ends up flooded and useless. Luckily, other industries move in and people make components for a new electronic device – the computer.

Meanwhile, in 1963, a huge car factory is built in Linwood, near Glasgow. An affordable car called the Hillman Imp is made there for an English-based company called Rootes.

Once, Scotland had successful home-grown motor companies such as Arrol-Johnston and Albion. But these have either died or been taken over.

Rootes, however, is given a lot of money by the government to build the factory near the Clyde because shipyards are closing and people need work. But after less than two decades Linwood is shut down, leaving 13,000 people unemployed.

Healing wounds

Soldiers who fought in the war and their families receive free medical care thanks to the greatest achievement of post-war Britain – the National Health Service, or NHS, which begins in 1948.

Many NHS patients benefit from penicillin, a medicine discovered by Scottish scientist Alexander Fleming. During the war, penicillin saved many lives – and afterwards saves millions more.

PLATFORM FOR THE FLOWERING OF THE HUMAN SPIRIT

ESCAPE FROM WAR

It's August 1947 and an audience of happy theatre-goers spills onto the street after a show at the very first Edinburgh Festival. This event proves Scotland can contribute something fresh and distinctive to British life after the war.

Festival performers are joined every year by amateurs who put on shows at the Festival Fringe, while film-makers exhibit at the Edinburgh Film Festival. With wartime food rationing still in force until 1954, the Edinburgh festivals are a welcome treat.

Meanwhile, a new generation of Scottish musicians, actors, comedians and other performers emerges. Although they

AND SCREEN

must often move to London or America to make it big, together they give the Scottish nation a voice on radio, film and television.

Audiences meanwhile enjoy international music, comedy, theatre and film in the ballrooms and theatres of Scotland's towns and cities. By the 1950s, many cinemas have been around for decades. Now they play host to an exciting new crop of films, increasingly in colour.

James Bond

During a high-stakes card game in a London casino in 1962, a man introduces himself as Bond – James Bond – and instantly becomes a legend. The fictional movie superspy is played seven times on screen by actor Sean Connery, from Edinburgh, who once worked as a milkman.

The man who created the character of James Bond, Ian Fleming, gives the secret agent a half-Scottish ancestry. Bond is partly inspired by wartime Commandos who trained in the Highlands – in particular three daring Scots: David Stirling, Fitzroy MacLean and Simon Fraser.

Home-grown talent

While international talent performs in Edinburgh, Glasgow produces many of Scotland's home-grown stars of comedy, music and film.

In the 1950s, comedian Chic Murray finds fame and is followed in the 1970s by Billy Connolly. Both men work in the Clyde shipyards before becoming comedians, and both are skilled at making hard-working people look on the bright side of life.

During this time, American-style pop music takes the world by storm, and Scotland produces its share of pop stars. In 1957 Glasgow-born singer Nancy Whiskey scores a hit with her version of the song 'Freight Train'.

Films about Scotland are often documentaries, about real-life, while some are made-up stories. The famous 1949 comedy *Whisky Galore* is based on a true event from 1941. It features war-weary Hebridean islanders saving bottles of whisky from a ship that has run aground.

Later home-grown Scottish films include *Gregory's Girl*, a hit comedy romance from 1980 about teenage life in the new town of Cumbernauld.

BLACK GOLD

It is winter 1975 and dawn is breaking over the North Sea a hundred miles east of Aberdeen. You are on an oil-production platform held high above the waves on massive legs of steel.

Oil and gas have recently been discovered here and now the race is on to pump out this 'black gold' – an essential fuel for heating and transportation.

Using a huge platform-mounted drill, oil is extracted from deep below the sea. It is then pumped to storage terminals such as Cruden Bay near Aberdeen and Sullom Voe in Shetland.

Aberdeen becomes Scotland's 'oil capital', taken over by oil-company offices and shipping. The industry makes some citizens rich but others gain little.

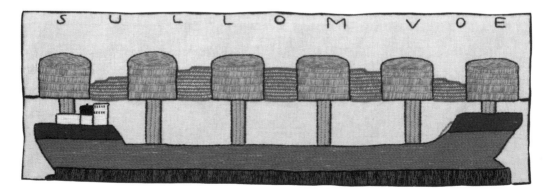

SEA OIL

EXCITEMENT AND DANGER

Work on oil rigs in the 1970s is exciting, exhausting and dangerous. To travel between neighbouring platforms or vessels, for example, workers are sometimes strapped into a harness called a bosun's chair. The chair, suspended by a line connecting the two decks, is launched into thin air. Sometimes gusts of wind twirl the chair about and waves loom up, covering the worker in ice-cold salt water.

Meanwhile, below the surface of the sea, divers risk their lives to ensure drilling apparatus and pipes are working properly. Oil and gas must be kept flowing even if the work is extremely hazardous.

Disaster strikes

In 1980, a Norwegian oil rig collapses and 123 people drown. Two years later, a rig near Newfoundland sinks killing 84. As lives continue to be lost, many people conclude that the oil industry puts profits before safety.

In 1988, the deadliest disaster happens when Piper Alpha, a platform in Scottish waters, explodes killing 167 workers. Major safety improvements are eventually made, but offshore workers and divers still earn 'danger money' due to the risks they have to take every day.

Dramatic protest

A vibrant stage play tours the country in 1974. *The Cheviot, the Stag and the Black, Black Oil* compares the story of Scotland's oil industry to the Clearances a century before. Its message is that while a few wealthy people profit, ordinary people lose out.

Winds of change

Economic and environmental fears about relying on oil and gas grow from the 1970s onwards. This creates interest in generating electricity from renewable sources such as wind power – a technology invented in Scotland by James Blyth in 1887.

SPORTING

ROOTS OF SUCCESS

By the late 20th century you can find parks, pitches, pools, courts, tracks and arenas in every corner of Scotland. These facilities help produce a stream of sporting heroes to inspire the nation.

The roots of Scottish success can be found at the first modern Olympics in Athens in 1896, where weightlifter Launceston Elliot wins gold. There follows a run of Olympic medallists including swimmers Ellen King and Sarah Stewart, and legendary runner Eric Liddell, in the 1920s.

At the 1924 Paris Olympics, Liddell says a prayer before running the 400-metre sprint with his head back and arms flailing to claim gold. He later works as a missionary in China helping the poor but is imprisoned during the war by the Japanese army, suffering greatly until his death in 1945.

HEROES

MODERN MARVELS

As a mark of respect to one of Scotland's greatest pre-war athletes, Edinburgh's Allan Wells crowns his gold in the 100-metre sprint at the 1980 Moscow Olympics by dedicating it to Eric Liddell. Wells's achievement is followed in 1991 by long-distance World Champion Liz McColgan, while swimming success peaks with David Wilkie's gold medal at Montreal in 1976.

Besides the Olympics, Wilkie wins the World Championships and Commonwealth Games – the last an event that Scotland hosts in 1970, 1986 and 2014. And the roll call of Olympic gold continues with the likes of sailor Shirley Robertson and cyclist Chris Hoy.

In the fields of extreme and dangerous sports, meanwhile, audacious 1960s Alpine mountaineer Dougal Haston and daring 1970s Formula One world champion Jackie Stewart are among a host of Scottish names that will be long remembered.

Victories and own goals

By the 1970s, football is by far Scotland's favourite sport. It brings the nation joy and heartache.

In Lisbon in 1967, Glasgow Celtic becomes the first British team to win the ultimate prize – the European Cup – under manager Jock Stein. Then, in 1972 and 1983, Rangers then Aberdeen win the UEFA Cup Winners' Cup.

Such achievements prompt a belief Scotland can win the 1978 World Cup in Argentina. Yet, despite a thrilling 3–2 victory over Holland, Scotland is knocked out in the opening round.

Historic triumph

In 2013 Scotland's Andy Murray becomes the first British men's Wimbledon champion since Fred Perry, 77 years previously.

DOWNFALL OF INDUSTRY

From the late 1960s, the clouds gathering over Scotland's shipyards, factories and coal mines burst. With Britain no longer an empire and other countries overtaking its economy, Scottish heavy industries are washed away as demand for their products disappears.

The launch of the *QE2* passenger liner by Queen Elizabeth in 1967 should be the crowning glory of generations of Clydebank shipbuilders, but instead marks the end of an era. The historic John Brown & Company yard that built her stops making ships soon after.

Like John Brown & Company, the Singer sewing machine factory and its workers survived the Clydebank Blitz to become industry leaders. But Singer, too, is devastated by competition and closes in 1980.

Elsewhere, the New Lanark textile mill, once a fine example of workers and bosses working together, is closed in 1968 and followed by Perthshire's Stanley Mills in 1989.

While some benefit from growth industries such as North Sea oil and whisky, communities that rely on traditional manufacturing suffer. Some outside companies are given money to build new factories in Scotland, but these government schemes often end in failures.

Many workers refuse to despair, however. Instead they take action.

THE TITANS

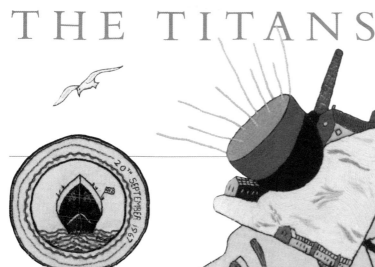

Workers fight back

In 1971, Glasgow's embattled Upper Clyde Shipbuilders somehow manage to fill their order book. Profits will come once the boats are built, but the British government refuses to loan the Scottish yards money to finish the orders.

Led by trade unionist Jimmy Reid and others, the shipbuilders vow to keep working anyway. Eventually public sympathy forces the government to help.

In the 1980s, the government vows to keep closing shipyards, factories and coal mines. In 1984, a miners' strike is called and soon mounted police are attacking miners with truncheons. The strike fails, the coal pits close and thousands lose their jobs.

Other major shutdowns include the vast Ravenscraig steel works in North Lanarkshire and the Timex electronics factory in Dundee. The mostly female Timex workers mount the last big strike of the era, and its failure closes a sad chapter in Scotland's history.

Broken nation

Scotland's self-confidence is shattered by the nation's industrial decline. Joblessness contributes to poverty and the break-up of families. Clydeside becomes the most unhealthy area in Europe with one of the highest rates of violent crime. Many wonder what can be done to turn the situation around.

GLASGOW IN STITCHES
RUCHAZIE RUCHAZIE
CALL THAT SINGING
HAMLET
WITCH HUNT
THE MAHABHARATA
GLASGOW MELA
BIRDS OF PARADISE
THE SHIP

But there are green shoots of hope. Ghostly shipyards are overgrown by the fragrant Glasgow Garden Festival and in 1990 the city becomes European City of Culture.

Poverty and ill health remain, but Glasgow shows things can be improved. Dundee is regenerated while Edinburgh becomes a UNESCO World Heritage Site.

The nation's artistic scene meanwhile crackles with confidence. The music of The Proclaimers and novels of Irvine Welsh, for example, talk about the despair and optimism of recent times using Scots words – just as Gaelic, too, is at last being used in the classroom.

REGENERATION

The thread of Scotland's history has brought you to the 21st century. The nation has regained confidence, taking greater control of its affairs.

Scotland's latest chapter begins around 1988 – the best and worst of times. The Piper Alpha disaster is followed by the bombing of a jumbo jet, which crashes into the village of Lockerbie killing 270 people.

A NATION DECIDES

In 1997 the nation votes to restore its parliament in Edinburgh. The Scottish Government takes control of areas such as health and education, and in 2004 a new parliament building is opened.

Giving Scotland more power has long been the aim of the Scottish National Party. Founded in the 1920s, the SNP gained 11 Members of Parliament in the House of Commons in London in 1974.

This success forced other political parties to act, resulting in the Scottish Parliament – but with ultimate power kept in London.

In 2014 another vote decides whether Scotland becomes independent.

Challenges ahead

Scotland's future is being shaped by many other factors, old and new.

The internet is changing everything. It has destroyed traditional jobs, but newer Scottish companies make some of the hottest digital products around.

Banking services remain key to Scotland's economy, but a financial crash in 2008 shows that unless bankers are regulated others suffer.

Tourists enjoy the Scottish landscape, but much of it is owned by a wealthy few while many cannot even afford a home.

Scots continue to emigrate, but new citizens move in. People still go to church, but many churches are now restaurants instead of prayer halls.

Scottish soldiers still wear kilts on parade and fight wars. But Scotland's historic regiments have almost disappeared, and the nation's main military asset is a controversial nuclear submarine base on the Clyde.

The world's first cloning of a mammal, Dolly the Sheep, was achieved near Edinburgh in 1996.

But global competition in 21st-century industries like bio-technology is fierce.

Success in this challenging world will depend on people like you.